Don't Pack…

Just *Move*!

The Plan, The Purpose, and The Power to Move forward

by

R. Michael Tarpley

CONTENTS

Acknowledgements

I want to thank God for His inspiration, for His speaking this book into my life, and for awakening me out of a deep sleep and allowing me to see His reality. This has been a journey, and without God I would have still been going through the motions of life and the ceremony of religion. Therefore, God I thank you for your faithfulness and the love that you continue to extend to me from day to day.

I want to thank my family, because next to God they are the reason I do everything. There is nothing that I would not do for my family, and likewise I know that there is nothing that they wouldn't do for me. I would like to give a special dedication to my wife who is nothing short of a miracle in my life. She inspires me to greatness, and challenges me daily to be better than the day before. Thank you for sacrificing our time together to allow me time to write this revelation. **LOVE YOU BABYKINS!** And of course, I thank my children, Dayvon, Geraldine, and Bielca, for your love that ignites my desire to be successful each and every day. **LOVE YOU TRIBE 7!** And to my grandchildren, Jaylah and Jonah, who drive me to leave a lasting legacy—I hope this make you proud. **POP POP LOVES YOU BOTH!**

To my Dad, you waited a long time for this. I know you enjoyed this as a sermon many years ago when I first preached this title. So here you go! **LOVE YOU POPPA BEAR!** And to my Mom, my biggest supporter in all things that I do, you are the greatest mother I could ever have! **LOVE YOU MOMMA**, KEEP BEING PEACHY!

Lastly, to my siblings, I have learned something great from each of you—from business to travel, to financial stewardship, to real estate investing, to faithfulness, to family unity, and to letting go of grudges and just having a good time ☺. **LOVE YOU ALL!**

Introduction

Thanks for joining the *move*ment.

The purpose and fundamental framework or focus, for "Don't Pack, Just *Move*" is at its core to motivate you, the reader, to move forward and accomplish your dreams and purpose for which you were created. Simultaneously, this book is equipped with instructions on how to go after your dreams and how to let go of the thing(s) that may have been holding you back.

Between the front and back covers of this book, you will find yourself exposed to an understanding of God that you likely have not experienced before. Through this understanding, I believe you will find yourself exposed to a clear picture of who God has called you to be.

Throughout most of our lives, we are often told that we should be "doing" something great, but too often we don't know what, and we are not given instructions on how and when. Well, I have good news for you, because "Don't Pack, Just *Move*" is a power-filled revelation that yields a deep, yet simple approach that will help you activate the "what," "how," and "when." This book kicks the door in for those who are seeking to do something they have never done before, and to aid those who are seeking to see their circumstances permanently changed.

If you are looking to learn how to move from pain to peace, or from paused to purpose, then it's way too early to put this book down. Without even knowing you at all, or knowing your position in life, I can say unequivocally that you have a level of greatness that has not yet been understood, believed, or even tapped into by you. If you are open and willing to receive the revelation in this book, then I believe that each and every chapter is going to take you one step further then the last step. By the time you get to the end of this book, you will have moved into a new place spiritually. Perhaps by the end of the reading, you may have moved emotionally, mentally, socially, and maybe even physically.

With a lot of what we are discussing in this book, you will typically hear the scriptures exposed in a manner that the church today will often overlook or simply sugarcoat. You will read things that will challenge both church leaders and church goers about their roles and responsibilities to God, themselves, their families, their communities, and the world. This is a ***MUST READ***, especially if you are tired of being confused about your purpose and how to get there. If you are tired of being scammed by people claiming to represent God, but are only after what God gave you, then again, this is a ***MUST READ***.

How did this book come about? This revelation came to me one day when I was evicted from an apartment early in my life. I was around

23 or 24 years old and had just started going back to church; I was trying to get my life together. I shared this apartment with a roommate. Prior to going back to church and getting my life together, we use to smoke weed, drink liquor, and have parties all the time—which is indirectly why we were evicted from the apartment.

We spent our money on the wrong things. Once I started going back to church, I heard God instruct me to move from where I was living. However, I didn't act on that instruction because I didn't think I had the financial ability to move. My goal at that point was simply to stay and work toward moving.

To make a long story short, while I was putting off making the move, one day the Marshalls showed up and removed everything from the apartment and put it all on the street corner. This, unfortunately, was not the first time I had been physically evicted, but it was definitely going to be the last time. It was in this instance that I learned God didn't need nor require me to pack, and He certainly didn't need me to wait until I "thought" it was the right time. **He only required me to do what he said**.

Of course, this book isn't suggesting that anyone should get evicted in order to move. In fact, most of what we will be sharing in these chapters is not about you physically moving at all, though for some of us that could also be the case. Nevertheless, how this book was birthed is

9

equally as important as its overall purpose. Therefore, my hope and belief is that this insight will cause you to be both uncomfortable *and* appalled, to the point that you will be forced into making a pivotal conscious decision—a decision whether to get up and MOVE from where you are, or to simply go back to sleep and stay where you have always been.

That said, I believe the content of this book, for many of its readers, is absolutely mission critical. Some are in such a crisis right now that you are spiritually suffocating and feel like you will not make it to your next breath if you don't quickly understand how to move forward. Others are vehemently desiring to see their full potential achieved in this life, and are sick and tired of being sick and tired. This book is for everyone, whether you are a believer in Christ Jesus or not. Maybe you have a weight problem that you need to get motivated to address, or maybe you have financial lack in your life. This book is a catalyst to help you get to the destination you have always felt you should reach. It will get you out of your layover and get you back on the plane. ***Come on, let's Move to chapter one…***

NOTE: Some scripture references may be used more than once throughout this book in order to further bring clarity to the revelation being shared.

CHAPTER ONE

"Sittin' on the dock of the bay …wasting time!"

On January 8, 1968, Otis Redding released a song entitled "(Sittin' On) The Dock of the Bay," which was written by Otis Redding and guitarist Steve Cropper. The lyrics of this song went something like this:

> *"Sittin' in the morning sun, I'll be sittin' when the evening comes.*
>
> *Watching the ships roll in, then I watch them roll away again, yeah...*
>
> *I'm sittin' on the dock of the bay, watchin' the tide roll away, ooh...*
>
> *I'm just sittin' on the dock of the bay **Wastin' time**."*

For some, these words are just lyrics to a song, but for others *(including myself earlier in life),* these words are a verbal depiction of exactly how we've chosen to live our lives. Our approach was simple: we just sat back in life and watched the proverbial ships roll in, and then in the same fashion watched them roll away again. No blood, sweat, or tears; no deep philosophy or complex plan to initiate. In fact, in order to be successful at this approach to life, one just has to sit back and do absolutely nothing.

As I just mentioned, there are many people who have adopted this approach to life, and the one consistency for those who have followed this approach has been that they have either felt that they have made virtually no movement in life, or in fact had made very little. As I began to look at the lyrics to this song, I could see the ships merely being verbal depictions that could be viewed as indicators of the opportunities afforded to us with which to make progress, to get ahead, to be successful, to fulfill our purpose, or to simply *MOVE*.

Now, there are some of us who have gotten comfortable with simply sitting, and just watching those around us obtain that which we have been sitting on the dock of the bay only dreaming about obtaining. We've watched *(and in some cases we are still watching)* these proverbial ships "roll in," and then watched them "roll away again," making little or no effort to get onboard. And then, those who won't get up will somehow muster up enough *nerve* to get upset, or even pray against everyone else who either did or were willing to get up.

These are some of the same folks that we find attempting to redirect blame from themselves for not making adequate moves in life. These are the same folks who redirect by putting the blame on their employers, their families, their government, their lack of role models, or even on God Himself. Every day, we see others get up from their "docks," pursue and obtain a better life for themselves and their families, and make a positive impact on the world. They innovate products, services, and organizations that improve the lives of many throughout the world, and yet those who sit on the dock of the bay "wastin' time" will hate, and feel that it's unfair that they, too, are not progressing in life.

Having said all of that, I am **NOT SAYING** that other factors don't make it more difficult for some to have success, because these factors **ABSOLUTELY** do. In fact, some of these, as well as other factors, can seem to slow your progress down to a point where you get the impression that you are actually going backward. This is where faith and pure grit and determination to participate in your own success have to be on full exhibit. Allow me to put this in an equation: ***Faith minus Works will always equal "the nonexistence of a belief to succeed."*** We will go in on this point in just a few.

To put the full spotlight on the revelation that I received from God through the lyrics to this song, it wasn't so much in the words "Sittin' on the dock of the bay;" rather, it was in the depressing phrase that follows, ***"wastin' time."*** See, "Sittin' on the dock of the bay" isn't in and of itself a bad thing; in fact, it can be extremely beneficial. You ask how? Well, at times it's good for us to sit, to be still, and get a firm understanding of who we are, where we are, and where we are going. At the same time, we need to be visualizing our dreams and desires, writing the vision and making it plain, because at its core, this earthly life is structured around time.

Ecclesiastes 3:1-2 *"To every thing there is a season, and a time to every purpose under the heaven: A time to be born, and a time to die; a time to plant, and a time to pluck up that which is planted;"* (KJV) (Please read verses 1 thru 11 of this text for a broader understanding.)

Most people do not have a good grasp of the reality that time was created to serve us, and not for us to serve time. Maximizing our time and not wasting it is our ability to own the time that has been given to us, and not be owned by the time. The truth is that too many of us have been or are still "wasting time," not willing to sacrifice what is needed to move ahead, nor applying the effort/work needed to see our reality changed for the better.

Allow me to put this another way: Many of us are sitting back and just saying "I'm waiting on God to do something" or "I'm not hearing God speak to me." Yet God is not re-doing, re-creating, or re-saying what He has already done, created, or said; IT'S NOT HAPPENING!!! So let's stop fooling ourselves and instead get to work and do what God has already said…

Psalm 62:11 *"God hath spoken once; twice have I heard this; that power belongeth unto God."* (KJV)

He has said it once, but the same thing has echoed again and again throughout the ages without the necessity of re-explaining or somehow evolving it's meaning to fit the times or our circumstances. The reason we are not hearing Him could simply be that we are looking for Him to merely agree with or regurgitate what we have told ourselves is the answer. Now, I'm not saying this is true in your case, but it's worth pondering within ourselves if we are going to make true progress.

I know some of you reading this may not believe in God. However, whether you believe or don't believe, it doesn't change the fact that you and I have been given time, talents, and gifts for use in this life to have true success. The time, talents, and gifts are most effective when these are used to help other people. In fact, the principle reason for us to have and use these things is to help others to understand and use their time, talents, and gifts as well. These things are not afforded to us to sit on and wait for someone else to activate or use on our behalf. We are empowered with these assets to MOVE, and therefore the only person you're truly waiting on is **you**. Others are only showing what can happen when you use what God has given to you, but they cannot use your time, talent, and gifts for you. As mentioned earlier, I believe the lyrics to "(Sittin' On) The Dock of the Bay" give some unique and unintentional insight that metaphorically speaks to how most of us, at times, have sat down on our potential and desires and limited ourselves from making significant progress in life.

This is not to say that those of us who have sat around and procrastinated

didn't desire to MOVE forward; perhaps it just means that some made an

unconscious choice to sit around and dream about moving forward, rather

than actually working to pursue and see their desires come to pass.

Proverbs 21:25 *"The desire of the slothful*

killeth him; for his hands refuse to labour." (KJV)

I believe that there is nothing worse than to have a dream, **AND**

the ability to accomplish the dream, but never get up and execute. That's

like saying "I wish I had $400,000,000," and you have the winning lottery

ticket in hand, but you won't get up and go present it to the lottery

officials in order to claim what is rightfully yours. HUH??? Who would do

that? I would submit to you that it's the same person who would say "I

want to be successful!" but does nothing to position him- or herself to

succeed, despite having the ability to perform at the highest levels. So

again, to bring this back full circle, the major challenge and/or dysfunction

is not the "sitting;" rather, it's when we find ourselves just *"**Wastin' time**"*

or simply sitting there too long.

There is a story in the bible that better articulates this topic and

gets to the heart of this chapter:

John 5:2-9 Vs. 2 *"Now there is at Jerusalem by the sheep market a pool, which is called in the Hebrew tongue Bethesda, having five porches.* **Vs. 3** *In these lay a great multitude of impotent folk, of blind, halt, withered, waiting for the moving of the water.* **Vs. 4** *For an angel went down at a certain season into the pool, and troubled the water: whosoever then first after the troubling of the water stepped in was made whole of whatsoever disease he had.* **Vs. 5** *And a certain man was there, which had an infirmity thirty and eight years.* **Vs. 6** *When Jesus saw him lie, and knew that he had been now a long time in that case, he saith unto him, Wilt thou be made whole?* **Vs. 7** *The impotent man answered him, Sir, I have no man, when the water is troubled, to put me into the pool: but while I am coming, another steppeth down before me.* **Vs. 8** *Jesus saith unto him, Rise, take up thy bed, and walk.* **Vs. 9** *And immediately the man was made whole, and took up his bed, and walked: and on the same day was the Sabbath."* (KJV)

Let me try to sum this up in the context of what we just read. There is a man sitting on a dock next to several other docks, which all were overflowing with folks who were impotent, blind, halt, and withered. Symbolically this is to say that some were powerless *(impotent)*, some had limited or no vision or direction for life *(blind)*, some had limited or no mobility to move forward *(halt)*, and others had altogether accepted that their hopes and dreams had shrunk and/or altogether dried up *(withered)*. The folks in this biblical text, as with many of us, were dealing with their own individual circumstances, in which "wastin' time" had only assisted them in getting worse, rather than enabling them to become better. Now, I want us to look at this more from a spiritual perspective than a physical one, because how we believe is actually how we operate as humans.

The text states that once a year a spiritual event would take place in the water, which was surrounded by the five docks/porches. The first person to get up from one of those docks, and MOVE into the water would then be cured of whatever circumstance that was keeping him/her on the dock. Thus, this annual event then becomes the ultimate motivator to all those who were sitting there on the docks to get up and do something— namely, to get up and move. This event would prove to separate those who believed that they could be healed of their circumstance *(to the point of participation)*, from those who may be merely sitting there "wastin' time."

The first point I would like to make in reaction to this scripture text is that **moving is the key!** Say it with me, Moving Is The Key! Now, though that's a strong and easily understood point, many of us still either altogether refuse to get up and move toward a better and brighter today/tomorrow, or we're allowing baggage to weigh us down and keep us from moving forward. This brings me to my second point, **Baggage cancels out desire!** Say it with me, Baggage Cancels Out Desire!

> **Hebrews 12:1-2** *"Therefore we also, since we are surrounded by so great a cloud of witnesses, let us lay aside every weight, and the sin which so easily ensnares us, and let us run with endurance the race that is set before us,"* **Vs. 2** *"looking unto Jesus, the author and finisher of our faith, who for the joy that was set before Him endured the cross, despising the shame, and has sat down at the right hand of the throne of God."* (KJV)

See, we may have a desire to move, but unless we lay aside every weight, that will likely not happen. The weight is those things that focus on what others might think, or puts focus on failures, or how hard it may be to stay the course until the end—this is that dead weight that never even lets us off the starting block, or in this case, off our "dock." And this keeps pulling on our inward motivation to keep us down. This could also be, for some, our arrogance to be something that we are not. ALL of this will need to be stripped from us so that we can RUN!!! Focusing on the author and finisher of our faith is the motivation that lets us know and convinces us to simply be who we were created to be, and to achieve what we were uniquely created to achieve. This in essence is freedom, this in essence is living without the proverbial packed bags.

In addition to laying aside every weight, we also must let go of the sin. That is to say, our unbelief in/doubt about God and about who God made us to be and what we were created to accomplish (be successful) within our purpose.

Having all of that in mind, it is important to note that it was not the physical limitations of those in the scripture text that kept them from succeeding; rather, I submit to you that it was their belief that they had to live within those limitations that kept them from succeeding. See, inward belief must come before any outward manifestation can be experienced.

Go with me for a moment. It was their belief that they could never get well, never be whole, or never make any significant progress in life. *THAT* was their baggage, and yet, it's sad to say, that it is far too often some of our baggage as well. Often, our baggage—particularly the packing of our baggage—can result in our being late, and/or altogether missing what may only be a few steps away from us receiving. Packing, or too much baggage, can at times cause a person to miss their bus, their plane, their train, or their "ship," essentially having them miss out on or greatly delaying their appointed greatness and destiny.

This biblical text makes yet another interesting point, though, and if you read over the text too quickly you may have missed it. The text states that the man had been on the dock and in his situation a ***long time***. Now, this is an important point and it had me thinking, would this man be spoken of in this text if he had only been in his situation for a short time? As you ponder that question, I think it would be a good time to mention that the bible makes several references that speak to life having many challenges and/or trials.

Job 14:1 *"Man that is born of a woman is of few days and full of trouble."* (KJV)

John 16:33 *"These things I have spoken unto you, that in me ye might have peace. In the world ye shall have tribulation: but be of good cheer; I have overcome the world."* (KJV)

Matthew 5:45 *"That ye may be the children of your Father which is in heaven: for he maketh his sun to* *rise on the evil and on the good, and sendeth rain*

on the just and on the unjust." (KJV)

2 Timothy 3:12 *"Yea, and all that will live godly in*

Christ Jesus shall suffer persecution." (KJV)

These challenges and/or trials are not foreign to any of us, which

simply means that they are not isolated to you, me, or any particular group

of people. Therefore, having that understanding, we can then intelligently

infer that everyone is subjected to the bad, **and** to the good that this life

has to offer. Taking all of this into account, and knowing that we all go

through challenges/circumstances, we can then couple that with the fact

that this man was in his circumstance a *long time*, and this should lead us

to the following conclusion: It's not necessarily a problem if we are found

in life to be "sittin' on the dock," or if we are found to have circumstances

and challenges.

None of this should be perceived as abnormal; in fact, based on the

scriptures that we just read, it is actually very normal and only becomes a

problem when we are found sitting on our proverbial "dock" for a ***LONG***

TIME! God is specifically calling that out in this text, which I believe

makes this very, very important. Remember, the first point in this

reference text analogy is that ***moving is the key!*** Therefore, if we are not

moving, it should be because we are using that time to get a firm understanding of who we are, where we are going and how we are going to get there. This should not take a long time. If the truth be told, I believe we should have gotten that understanding by the time the next ship would have pulled into our port.

There is truly no delay or interruption between the revelation and the execution of or participation in what has been revealed for us to do, or where it is for us to go. If you miss your "ship," you have to wait for the next ship. This is what would be considered, according to the focus scripture text, "a long time" and, according to the song lyrics, "wastin' time."

Now I should make a very important, yet obvious, statement: time is not something that we're able to get back in life, nor are we able to guarantee it for ourselves tomorrow, thus it has to be maximized at all times (no pun intended). This moment, this point in time, is all we have. We have to make a "now" choice whether to live where we have always been, or **MOVE** to where we have always wanted to be. We can choose to wait for "time" to do something for us, or we can choose to do something in the time with which we have been afforded. A former Pastor and mentor of mine use to ask, "When is faith?"

Hebrews 11:1 "<u>NOW FAITH</u> is the <u>substance of</u> <u>things hope for, and the evidence of things not</u> <u>seen</u>…" (KJV)

Faith is always NOW!

Our focus scripture text mentions that Jesus saw a certain man sitting on a porch by a pool (*sittin' on the dock of the bay*), having no name mentioned, which frankly just means that it could have been any one of us. He saw that this certain man had been on the porch or on the dock in the same state for **a long time**, so He simply said to this certain man (paraphrasing), "Do you even want to be well?" In other words, do you want to change? Do you want to move into your purpose and into a better life for you and your family? Do you have any "get up" in you, any drive in you to leave from your dock? This was not a question for yesterday, or a question for tomorrow, this was a "now" question, and it required a "now" response.

Please pay attention to this next point: although Jesus was asking the man a question, He was just setting him up to give him revelation. That said, it is equally important to recognize that at the time of revelation, it is simultaneously the time to move. Remember what we just said earlier, that *there is truly no delay or interruption between the revelation and the execution/ participation of what has been revealed for us to do, or where it is for us to go."*

Now don't miss this. Jesus ultimately said, do you want to be better than what you are today? And the obvious inward answer in all of us is, "Of course I want to be better," and that comment would be the beginning of our revelation, and subsequently our change. The revelation is "HOW"—how do I become better? That starts with a desire to be better, and while having that understanding, we then simultaneously believe we can be better and that the time is NOW for us to move. The fact that we "want to be better" is the inward indicator that we believe that there is a "better," and this all activates the external display of our faith and works to achieve what we now know "better" to look like.

Like many of us, I don't believe that this certain man had any real desire to stay in the state that life had left him in, so he said, *(paraphrasing)* "I've tried, but my efforts alone have only brought me to where you've found me." Jesus, hearing this man's heart and not his words, said to him three key things: **1)** *Rise*, **2)** *take up your bed*, and **3)** *walk.*" And then in the very next verse, the bible indicates that there were three key responses. This certain man **1)** was immediately healed, **2)** he took up his bed, and **3)** he walked.

The latter two tasks are not difficult as long as the first task takes place, but if the first task doesn't happen, then the other two tasks will be found to be impossible. Jesus said "Rise" (this was the first task), and the response was that this certain man was immediately healed. This was the revelation to this certain man, and perhaps to someone reading this now. "How do I become better?" Jesus said, "Rise!"

Please take note that Jesus in this text did not say to the man that "You are healed," although healing certainly took place. Instead, He said to this certain man, "Rise!" I believe this was said to reveal to us that when Jesus is present, our healing is already there; we only have to accept and/or access it by faith. However, our faith as it relates to our belief in God and who God made us isn't enough; we also have to *demonstrate* what we believe. In other words, we still need to respond/ **to move**/ to participate in what we want to see and experience in this life.

James 2:20. *"But wilt thou know, O vain man, that faith without works is dead?"* (KJV)

You must have some actions that essentially back up your claim that you believe. In my attempt to further bring clarity to this point, let me say this: it's not our works that bring about the healing of our circumstances; our works only display outwardly what we've already believed and witnessed our reality to be inwardly. If we believe it, then we can work it.

Now, I hear some of you saying that when Jesus said "Rise," and then the text said that the man was immediately healed, this merely means that when God speaks, His word simultaneously responds to itself making whatever He said to immediately come to pass. However, I would submit to you that it's not really about God "making" His word come to pass for us; rather, it's more about us <u>accessing</u> by faith/ belief what His word has <u>already</u> declared and accomplished concerning our lives.

Some will likely struggle a little with that, but I promise that as we go along from chapter to chapter, this point will become even more clear. Let me just say this, God's word is His word. It doesn't change. God is not saying anything new. As I said earlier, He has said it once, but the same thing is echoed again and again, rather than the meaning being re-explained or somehow evolving over time. That being the case, God is not just sitting back waiting for us to mess up so that He can say something new, or perhaps create a new way for us to get out of wherever we are. He is not "making a way;" rather, He is "The Way" <u>already</u>.

> **John 14:6** <u>"Jesus saith unto him, **I am the way,** the truth, and the life: no man cometh unto the Father, but by me.</u>" (KJV)

God's word is the same yesterday, today, and forever (Hebrews 13:8) and the Word is just sitting there throughout all ages <u>waiting for us</u> to believe enough to access it, and to simultaneously get up and possess what His word has made available for us…so **GET UP AND MOVE!**

Look, no one attempts to sit in a seat unless they first believe that the chair is there. And no one tries to turn on a TV unless they first have a belief that the TV will display a picture. The point isn't whether the TV comes on or not; the point is that we have to have a measure of faith (a glimpse of expectation) before there is any display of works. So, though we may not know in all cases what will happen, we do know that with a small measure of faith <u>something will</u>.

This brings us back to instruction and response, or revelation and participation. When we hear the revelatory word such as "Rise," it increases our faith and we then have the choice to accept or not accept the fact that we can "Rise" and get up.

> **Romans 10:7** *<u>So then faith comes by hearing, and hearing by the word of God</u>.*" (KJV)

Not before, and not after, but at the same time that I believe, I then also harness the power to begin to work that very belief. Again, not before, and not after, as if there is some sort of foresight or delay of uncertainty about what we believe, but in the "now" moment.

In this moment, we are getting up out of our long-time condition. In this moment, we are saying goodbye to the past. In this moment, we are at the top of our game. In this moment, we will not be late for the ship, the plane, or the bus. We are saying that we will not allow our circumstances to dictate and/or control how we live. So, for example, when I understand and believe that I am the lender and not the borrower…

> **Deuteronomy 15:6** *"For the LORD thy God blesseth thee, as he promised thee: and thou shalt lend unto many nations, but thou shalt not borrow; and thou shalt reign over many nations, but they shall not reign over thee."* (KJV)

> **Proverbs 22:7** *"The rich ruleth over the poor, and the borrower is servant to the lender."* (KJV)

…then I must, at the same time, begin living/working out my belief. If not, then it will honestly show that I don't truly believe that I am the lender. There is no gray area.

At the time that I believe, I may be in debt, I may even be broke, but at that time (if I truly believe), I must move in the direction of my belief. And yet, somehow I can still hear someone saying, "What does all that mean?" It means that from this moment on, I can no longer dwell on how I loosely handled my finances in the past, or what my financial position was yesterday. Rather, <u>at the moment I believe</u>, I must begin to move forward by surrounding myself with like-minded people, balancing

my checkbook, making consistent payments to my creditors, wisely

investing my money, not making new debt, and putting myself (and my

family) in a position to be a help to others.

It means that from this moment on, I can no longer eat like it

doesn't matter and ignore my body's warning signs. Rather, <u>at the moment</u>

<u>I believe</u> that I can be healthier, I must begin to move forward by

surrounding myself with like-minded people, exercising regularly,

watching what I eat, when I eat, and how much I eat, and putting myself

(and my family) in a position to be a help to others. If I've been told I have

diabetes, then I can't just pray for it to go away; I must also put down the

Ho Ho's cakes, the donuts, the crème brulèe, as well as the sodas and

sweet teas. I must choose to activate my self-control to see myself become

better.

Remember, faith without works is dead—it simply doesn't exist.

When you first realize that something is possible, it's <u>at that moment</u> that

you accept the power to make it possible. So yes, it is what you do with

that power that will indeed work out your successes and purpose.

Again…*it is important to note that it was not the physical limitations of*

those in the text that kept them from succeeding; rather I submit to you that it was their belief that they had to live within those limitations that kept them from succeeding."

Now, I've said all that to say this: What we often, and sometimes intentionally, miss in God's word to us is that even though God is able to do **any**thing, He still requires us to do **some**thing. This certain man had to get up. Yes, God's word revealed the healing that was available to this man; however, the man himself **had to get up** (use the power that God had given him) if he wanted to go forward and fully experience his change. It's one thing to *be* healed; it's another thing to *live* healed! Immediately this certain man got up, because I believe he wanted to *live* healed, and not just *be* healed. If he wanted to just *be* healed, he would have just remained lying there knowing that he was healed, knowing that he was now better, having the ability to move, but consciously choosing to stay where he was.

Now, if we are to be honest with ourselves, how many of us are choosing not to move, even though we now know we have the ability to move and live a better life? Here's another personal question that I have for you: Do you want to LIVE, or do you want to just BE?? (Jesus said to the man, "Wilt thou be made whole?"—in laymen's terms, "Do you want to live, I mean really live?") Can you look at yourself in the mirror knowing that you have the ability to move, but <u>YOU</u> choose to sit on the dock of the bay, wastin' time? Do you have the winning lottery ticket, but refuse to get up and present it to the lottery officials? It is in you, and in all of us, to be great, but we **<u>must</u>** participate in our own success. I'm going to say that one more time: It is in you, and in all of us, to be great, but we **<u>must</u>** participate in our own success.

> **Ephesians 3:20-21** "*<u>Now unto him that is able to do exceeding abundantly above all that we ask or think, according to the power that worketh in us,</u>* **Vs. 21** <u>*Unto him be glory in the church by Christ Jesus throughout all ages, world without end. Amen.*</u>" (KJV)

The "power" spoken of in this text speaks about the "faith" that works on the inside of believers, to bring that which is unseen into the natural realm which is seen. Make no mistake, the greater purpose, and/or our exceeding abundance, comes from "The Word" at work in us by way of faith in Him. And that faith, coupled with outward works, is what allows our victory to be manifested.

> **Matthew 13:58** "*<u>And he did not many mighty works there because of their unbelief.</u>*" (KJV)

James 2:20 *"But wilt thou know, O vain man, that faith without works is dead?"* (KJV)

This focus text eloquently speaks to the title of this book, "Don't Pack, Just *Move*," by simply saying that this certain man, *which could be any of us*, took up his bed (his testimony) and moved. **Don't miss this last point!!** He didn't leave the same person that he was when he got there. Instead, he now believed something different. And when we look at the core of who we are, and who God created us to be, we will then begin to understand, and walk in what we believe.

This certain man took his "testimony" (his bed), which was an illustration and/or further proof of the victory that he had now accepted and had begun living. His carrying the bed says to all those who knew him before that, 'Yes, I am that guy who was on the dock, but I'm now better; I have found **"The Way"** to beat this, I have overcome, I have won!" And even though he took the bed and left, he did not pack his past, his former way of thinking, his circumstance(s)/ condition(s); he did not take back with him a defeated mindset. He did not leave saying, "I tried to get to the pool, but someone beat me to it," or "I don't have anyone to help me." He didn't leave broken; rather, this certain man left as someone who was now whole, complete, alive, believing that he didn't have to live another day the way he was living on the dock. Thus, he **moved**. He came to the dock needing help from others, but he left the dock with the ability within his limbs to help himself and others.

One of the main reasons why some of us have not gotten up, and will not get up out of our long-time conditions, is because we keep surrounding ourselves with people who are satisfied with their long-time conditions. These people create workarounds and excuses for their circumstances and conditions instead of saying, "This is the last day I'm going to feel sorry for myself," "This is the last day I'm going to accept defeat," "This is the last day I'm going to allow others to talk me out of my dreams." We keep these people in our lives not because we are trying to help them; rather, because they help us to justify how we feel about our own failures and our own insecurities. This certain man moved from those who sat around him on those docks, who helped him to reinforce that defeated way of thinking that he had been carrying.

If you're someone that has not allowed yourself to be around go-getters, or around those who will challenge you to be better and do things that you've never done before, then let me encourage you to get those people in your life. **Don't Pack, Just *Move*! NOW!!** This certain man stopped wasting time and left his dock with the ability to walk, to be mobile, to move from one point in life to another, because he no longer

35

carried his old baggage (beliefs, ideas, struggles, negative people, etc.). He didn't pack, he simply moved.

The chapter **"Sittin' on the dock of the bay ...wasting time!"** is something that I believe we all can relate to, and likely have related to at some point in time in our lives. Some may even feel like you are on the dock right now wastin' time. To you, I want to take this moment and give you a specific word that will help you move forward, and that word is **"Rise!"**

You are the lender, and not the borrower *(Deuteronomy 28:12)* / You are above only, and never beneath *(Deuteronomy 28:13)* / You are first, and not last *(Matthew 20:16)* / You are the head, and not the tail *(Deuteronomy 28:13)* / You are more than a conqueror *(Romans 8:37)* / You are an overcomer by the blood of Jesus, and by the word of your own testimony *(Revelation 12:11)* / You can do all things through Christ *(Philippians 4:13)* / You are fearfully, and wonderfully made *(Psalm 139:14)* / No weapon formed against you will be able to prosper *(Isaiah 54:17)* / What shall we then say to these things? If God be for us, who can be against us? *(Romans 8:31)*

NOW! IF YOU FEEL YOU'RE WASTING TIME, THEN DON'T WASTE ANOTHER MOMENT; *"RISE!"* GET UP OFF THE DOCK

THAT YOU'VE BEEN CLINGING TO FOR SO LONG! GET ON THAT SHIP THAT IS HEADING OUT TO SEA AND REMEMBER THAT WHEN YOU DO RISE FROM YOUR CIRCUMSTANCE, ***<u>DON'T PACK</u> anything, <u>JUST</u> begin to <u>MOVE</u>!!!***

CHAPTER TWO

"To _Get_ what you Want, you have to _Get_ what you _Got_"

As with the last chapter, I would like to introduce a focus scripture text that will help better illustrate the point I'm about to make. Before we dive into this, please allow me to expound a little on the title of this chapter, **"To Get what you Want, you have to Get what you Got."** This title is a simple play on the word "GET"; To **GET** *(to obtain)* what you want, you have to **GET** *(having understanding of)* what you **GOT** *(what you already have)*.

Having this in mind, let's go…

Our scripture text for this chapter comes out of Luke 15, which has a traditional theme of "the lost being found." This will add just a little more flavor and color toward helping us to better understand the overall topic and context of this book.

> **Luke 15:11-20 Vs. 11** *"And he said, A certain man had two sons"* **Vs. 12** *"And the younger of them said to his father, Father, give me the portion of goods that falleth to me. And he divided unto them his living."* **Vs.13** *"And not many days after the younger son gathered all together, and took his journey into a far country, and there wasted his substance with riotous living."* **Vs. 14** *"And when he had spent all, there arose a mighty famine in that*

land; and he began to be in want." **Vs. 15** *"And he went and joined himself to a citizen of that country; and he sent him into his fields to feed swine."* **Vs. 16** *"And he would fain have filled his belly with the husks that the swine did eat: and no man gave unto him."* **Vs. 17** ***"And when he came to himself, he said, How many hired servants of my father's have bread enough and to spare, and I perish with hunger!"*** **Vs. 18** ***"I will arise and go to my father,*** *and will say unto him, Father, I have sinned against heaven, and before thee,* **Vs. 19** *And am no more worthy to be called thy son: make me as one of thy hired servants."* **Vs. 20** ***"And he arose,*** *and came to his father. But when he was yet a great way off, his father saw him, and had compassion, and ran, and fell on his neck, and kissed him."*

Allow me to summarize what we just read by saying this: Just like Lemony Snicket, the text that we read illustrates this young man's series of unfortunate events. It helps illustrate the catalyst that drives home a crucial revelation that helped this young man to open his spiritual/ inner eye. Now this young man, as well as those reading this text, draws from both the catalyst and the revelation. This is done in spite of the physical place that we may find ourselves in at the time of the revelation. Now, I know what you are saying," Catalyst? Revelation? What are you talking about?" Well, let's break this all down...

The text states that a father has two sons and one (the younger son) says to his father, *(paraphrasing)* "I'm tired of waiting for you to die, so give me my inheritance now so I can live the way I want to live." And though this man was young, he seemingly felt that he had life all figured out; he believed he knew what it would take to live a sustainable life.

Question: Is it possible that some of us, while young, may have had the same thought that we seemingly knew what it would take to live a sustainable life? As you ponder that, let me keep going…

Now, after the father heard his younger son's request, he then, with all the love in his heart for his two sons, had compassion and perhaps had felt compelled to split his wealth (his two son's inheritance) and give the younger son what he was requesting. And almost immediately upon receipt, just about the middle of the week, the younger son gathered his things, left his family, and journeyed to another country. Once on his own, the story lets us know that before long the son had spent every penny that his father had given him on riotous *(lawless/ rebellious)* living, and thus he was left flat broke. And just as he was simultaneously facing one of the most unfamiliar, frightening, and challenging situations of his young life, the text tells us that yet another matter arises. It seems that the country in which he chose to live was experiencing a famine; that is to say a food shortage. This, then, truly becomes a series of unfortunate events. Now that he has no money and no food, his self-preservation kicks in and he decides to get a job feeding pigs. However, in doing so he gets nothing for his efforts, and even though he would have eaten the corncobs in the pigs' slop, no one would even give him permission to do that.

This brings us to a crucial and pivotal point in the story of this young man's life, where he found himself at rock bottom; he was lost, starving, and broke *(financially, physically, socially, and emotionally)*. He was literally smelling like a pig, and was in desperate need to be in a different environment than where he had found himself at in that moment. Before I lay this out further, let me ask you a question: Have you ever been in a place that not only felt bad and was miserably uncomfortable, but it also gave off such a smell/ stench (metaphorically speaking) that it literally brought you to your knees?

To be clear, I'm not talking about smells that may have emanated from a physical location; I'm talking more about the internal odor of your circumstance and issues that have infiltrated your life. This is a stench that reeks at a much higher level than the awful physical stench of a pig pen.

The smell of a pig pen can possibly make you throw-up, but the odor and stench of your circumstance can often be so overpowering that it can make you cry, faint, or even drive you to the point of wanting to take your own life. This young man, like maybe some of us, was in that moment! We should understand that he was very badly out of place, he had no friends where he was, he had no money, he had no food, and his hope of survival was rapidly dwindling. This in and of itself does not necessarily cause this level of stench, this level of stench can be attributed to you being the origin of your sorrow or when your actions are what led you to this point. Now tell me, does this sound remotely similar to that raunchy, rotting, smelling place that you may have once found yourself in, or that you are in right now? If so, then listen closely to this next point.

At the time that the life within this man was fading rapidly, and he had all but lost his identity, the text says something utterly profound. It says that ***<u>he came to himself…</u>*** It was at THAT MOMENT that he realized from whence he had come. He came from something much greater and higher than where he had found himself living. In short, I believe something inside of him began to awaken, and he said to himself, "You don't belong here, you are better than your circumstance!" He realized that everything he seemed to have lost—money, food, family, and self-esteem—all still existed for him, just not in the place where he found himself settling. That moment reminded him of not only who his father was, but also the totality of what his father had for him and his brother to inherit. Remember, to **GET** *(to obtain)* what you want, you have to **GET** *(understand)* what you **GOT** *(what you already have)*.

Selah *(stop and consider that for a moment)…*

<*Commercial Break…*>

Always understand that your circumstances come to help **you** find **you**, so that you can then both recognize and maximize the power and purpose given to you as your inheritance. It's this power, this inheritance, that not only reminds us of who we are, but equally important, it is also the catalyst that helps us to get out of our pig pens.

> **Ephesians 3:20** *"Now unto him that is able to do exceeding abundantly above all that we ask or think, **according to the power that worketh in us**,"* KJV

> **Deuteronomy 8:18** *"But thou shalt remember the Lord thy God: for it is **he that giveth thee power to get wealth**, that he may establish his covenant which he sware unto thy fathers, as it is this day."* KJV

<*…and we're back*>

This young man had started to remember that he came from something special, something greater than where he had found himself. And it is at this moment of clarity that he knew he was better than that pig pen he was in, he knew that he was better than how he was allowing people to treat him, and he knew he was better than the actions that caused him to be there in the first place. Figuratively put, this man woke up from the nightmare he had been recently living and I believe his first thought when he awoke was, "Why am I here?" Not so much a question of how he came to be there, but rather more of a question of "Why am I *still* here, considering that I come from so much greater than this?"

Have you ever suddenly realized that you come from greatness? Maybe you considered this while you were in a really bad moment in your life, perhaps while tears were flowing down your cheeks and your head was ready to explode due to a high level of stress. Maybe it was that time when you were being evicted from your residence, and then realized that it was only due to your own irresponsible and careless actions. Maybe you were on drugs, or in a toxic relationship that you felt you couldn't live without. Perhaps your business was failing because you stopped learning, thinking that you knew enough to always be successful. In any case, right at that very moment something inside you reminded you of where you came from; it reminded you that you not only had the ability to be great, but perhaps you also denied the support needed to be great.

For some of us, these are not just hypothetical examples, these are stories of our lives! **And the most intense, liberating, and thought-provoking part of all of this is what we do when we realize that we don't come from where we find ourselves currently dwelling**. Once you realize that you come from greatness, you will then begin to arrive at the <u>answer</u> and <u>solution</u> to your rhetorical question, "Why Am I Here?" Wherein, you will arrive at the only real viable <u>answer</u>, which is simply that *you forgot who you are*. You will also arrive at the only real viable <u>solution</u>, which is merely to get up, and get out of where you know you don't belong (and to do it quickly).

In other words, "Don't Pack, Just *Move*!" and hurry yourself to the place where you know you belong. That successful place, that peaceful place, that place that helps you to shout when everyone else is quiet. That place that makes you sing when you can't even carry a note. That place that makes you laugh when nothing around you is even remotely funny. That unique place that can make you dance even when there is no music playing. This place is not so much an outward place than an inward place. Oh yes, there is an inward place we can go to that doesn't actually require for us *(at that moment)* to leave the physical place in which we are currently located. As a matter of fact, let me make this point clear by saying that you can't even get to a new outward place until you have gone there already inwardly/ spiritually. This young man in the text "came to himself;" he allowed himself to be reminded of who he was, and this was an inward moment which ultimately sparked an outward change in location.

> **Vs. 20 "_And he arose, and came to his father_. _But when he was yet a great way off, his father saw him, and had compassion, and ran, and fell on his neck, and kissed him_."**

Let me say this: If you don't know who you are, the devil *(and/or those around you who may influence you)* will convince you to be whoever they want you to be. You can't allow yourself to not know or simply forget who you are, where you come from, and from whom you come. It is vitally important in order to move forward. Now, I'm not talking about your physical place, your high school, your hometown, or even your blood family; those can certainly be fixations that are "all good" and maybe even deserving of a measure of self-satisfaction. However, I'm talking about a deeper appreciation, one that stems back to who created you, and the purpose for which you have been created. This is not about how smart your family is, how many degrees are in your family, how many business owners, or how much money your family may have or not have. This is about something that is deep within you, something that others can't see with their physical eyes. Something that may or may not have shown up in your family or in your circle of friends, yet it is unique to you and individually yours, so make no mistake: **YOU ARE BORN FOR SOMETHING GREAT!**

Don't let anyone, or any circumstance challenge you to the point that you accept being a lower version of yourself or accept that you have to dwell in a physical or metaphoric pig pen. As we observe the young man in the text going back to his father, it is indicative and symbolic of us humbly going back to God—not physically going to God, but in mind and spirit going back to Him after we've lost our way and have forgotten our identity; when we have somehow gotten off course and found ourselves asking "Why am I here?" It's in those times that we must snap out of it, wake up and refocus, because following the crowd or our own clouded thoughts can get us lost and have us doing things we had no intention of doing.

That said, most of us, if we are honest with ourselves, have had dreams of being on some higher level by this time in our lives. We intended to be a lot further along in life *(whatever that may have meant to each of us individually)*. See, we wanted to be in one place, but instead we found ourselves in another. We're "sittin' on the dock of the bay, wastin' time!", or better yet, we're not "obtaining what we want because we can't seem to understand, or grasp, what we already have" (this is everything!). Therefore, it is that much more important for us to know how to get to that desired place, rather than "wastin' time" on the dock of the bay not understanding the power and purpose we already have to move forward. This power is required in order for us to change our thinking from one way of thinking to another, to get us to where we know we should be living.

We all know that with every good success story, there has to be a point of change. That is to say a point of transition, that pivotal point that gives way to our "success." After all, we have heard that the very definition of insanity is doing the same thing but expecting different results. Therefore, without "transition" all we are left with is insanity. Considering that fact, permit me to reiterate that, it's not as important to move physically as it is important to move mentally and spiritually. Because if you move physically and don't move spiritually, you will likely return to repeat your experience(s), but if you move spiritually *and* physically, then the only way you will return is with great success to help others out of their pig pen.

Most of the time when we find ourselves in a messy self-inflicted or socially-inflicted circumstance, we don't readily have the resources to physically move, but what we can do is refocus our mind and spirit to mentally and spiritually move. See, I don't always have to physically leave town in order to get away from other people's "I can't, so you can't" mentality, or their reckless approach to life. I can be sitting right next to a person at work, or on the bus, or even at church, but be as far from that person as the east is from the west. Now, that's not to say I should physically stay near this person for *"a long time,"* as in our discussion in chapter one. However, if I focus myself to achieve greatness, then even while that person is in my presence I will not allow him/her to influence me, or take me away from being great.

Let me explain: I can be inwardly free until I'm in position to be physically free. Your cubicle may be next to him/her at work now, but it doesn't mean that you have to accept their negative remarks or join in with their gossip. Now, I probably just touched a nerve with those comments, because some of us may be just waking up to the fact that you are in a pig pen, and are asking yourself "Why am I here?" When you get to the point of asking "Why am I here?", it's important that you understand you had to have already arrived at the conclusion that you don't belong there. This is a very important point, so let me say that again for all those in the cheap seats… *When you get to the point of asking "Why am I here?", it's important that you understand you had to have already arrived at the conclusion that you don't belong there.*

Many of us may be in pig pens that we should simply not be attached to: certain jobs, a bad financial state, unhealthy relationships, or perhaps participating in some non-edifying "prosperity" preaching church. When we awaken to the fact that we come from better, and better is expected of us, then it's at that very moment that we realize that WE ARE BETTER. This is a simple philosophy that says if I come from greatness, then I, too, must be great!

> *Vs. 17 "**And when he came to himself,** he said,*
>
> *How many hired servants of my father's have bread*
>
> *enough and to spare, and I perish with hunger!"*

To **GET** *(to obtain)* what you want, you have to **GET** *(understand)* what you **GOT** *(what you already have)*.

I hope this is beginning to settle in your spirit, because I do feel that at this point someone is getting it now.

Having said all of that, let's pivot from the question "Why am I here?" to the questions "Where should I be?" and "How do I get there?" Let's look at another text below to help further expound on this reality…

51

Isaiah 52:1-2 Vs. 1 *"<u>Awake, awake; put on thy strength, O Zion; put on thy beautiful garments</u>, O Jerusalem, the holy city: for henceforth there shall no more come into thee the uncircumcised and the unclean."* **Vs. 2** <u>*Shake thyself from the dust; arise,*</u> *and* <u>**sit down**</u>, *O Jerusalem:* <u>**loose thyself from the bands of thy neck**</u>, *O captive daughter of Zion."* (KJV)

In this text, the prophet Isaiah is speaking the word of God to God's people at a time when they were in captivity to the Babylonians. Let's look at this from its overall holistic and practical nature. From this text, we receive some very critical points on getting out of some of our circumstances that we admittedly got ourselves into with our own foolish desires.

James 1:14 *"<u>But every man is tempted, when he is drawn away of his own lust, and enticed</u>."* (KJV)

The ***first critical point*** raised in Isaiah 52 is "<u>Awake, awake!</u>" This is a prerequisite/ requirement to being free of our circumstance and to be able to move forward in life. The only way you can clearly see that you are in a "pig pen" *(per our first focus text in Luke 15)* is to WAKE UP! Now, this prerequisite is mentioned twice—"Awake, awake"—which would indicate that if we are in a "pig pen," or a really bad circumstance of our own doing, then we are indeed in a deep sleep and are living life unconsciously. Living life asleep is not living at all; in fact, truly living requires us to participate, and participation requires us to be conscious. If we awaken to find ourselves in a "pig pen" of our own making, we then realize that it's not God, nor our parents, nor anyone else that put us there, but we ourselves have dozed off and fallen asleep at the wheel of life. Just the same, we should be ever so mindful that when we awake and utilize the gifts, talents, and purpose that have been given to us for "success" in life, we must allow them to place us in a position to help others.

The ***second critical point*** raised in this text was "<u>Put on your strength</u>!" This point indicates that once we are awakened, as it was with the children of Israel in this text, it is also then required that we participate/ get involved with our own success. In short, once we gain awareness of who we are and from where/whom we come, then it is at this time that we **MUST** be confident and courageous, and do something that aligns with that awareness. Do something with what you **"GOT"**! You have strength, then put it on!

53

> **James 2:20** *<u>But wilt thou know, O vain man, **that**</u>*
>
> *<u>faith without works is dead</u>?"* (KJV)

The ***third critical point*** that is raised is "<u>Put on thy beautiful</u>

<u>garments</u>!" As with all of these points from this text in Isaiah, this speaks

to the children of Israel coming out of captivity and becoming free of their

bondage. This obviously ties back into the original focus text of this

chapter in Luke 15; as well, it speaks to our own deliverance from

bondage. This critical point declares that we have to put on our best,

which implies that we have to take off our worst, our mediocre. We have

to take off our old rags, our old ways, our old ideas, which are ultimately

our baggage, and we have to put on what aligns and eventually speaks to

our destiny.

> **Galatians 3:26-27 Vs. 26** *<u>For ye are all the</u>*
>
> *<u>children of God by faith in Christ Jesus</u>."* 27 *"<u>For</u>*
>
> *<u>as many of you as have been baptized into Christ</u>*
>
> *<u>have put on Christ</u>."* (KJV)

The ***fourth critical point*** that was raised is "<u>Shake thyself from the</u>

<u>dust</u>!" As this relates to the text, and to our own transition from captivity,

this point gives us the understanding that the days of feeling sorry for ourselves, and simply wishing things were different, are now over. It's time now to participate and move forward to change, to experience the beauty of life. Sure, there are plenty of people who would like to keep us covered up and buried in dirt, and if the truth be told, some of them are the ones who hurled some of that dust/dirt on us in the first place. Then again, I'm sure this is not a surprise to any of you. After all, misery loves company!

There are some who want others to look, smell, and feel dirty in order to make themselves seem clean. Their philosophy is, the dirtier I can make you look, the purer I feel about myself, and the better I can project that very image to others. Don't let people keep dirt on you! Shake thyself from the dust; accept that you belong to, and come from, your Heavenly Father and you are delivered from your past sins and mistakes. And if you are delivered, and only if you are delivered, you can then talk about what you use to be and do so without having any shame. Therefore, no one else can throw that dirt back upon you and hurt you or shame you. As a matter of fact, you can be free to talk about your past yourself, which will proactively take the sting out of their attacks before they can mount one against you. Just accept Christ, and you can be free to let them talk and throw dirt. They can say what they want because you've shaken that dust off already.

Think of it this way: If you don't have dirt on you to begin with, then you force people to have to talk about what you do have on you. *Selah...*

The ***fifth critical point*** that was raised is "<u>Arise!</u>" For me, these last three points are the most telling of a person's transition and/or awakening. "Arise!" simply demands that a person GET UP! It demands that a person TAKE AUTHORITY! If a person is truly sick and tired of being sick and tired, then he/she will GET UP and MOVE to be better. The two choices that are presented to you when you awake are to either get up and maximize the hours that are given to you in that day, **OR** you can quite simply go back to sleep. Yet, going back to sleep has never produced any measure of success; it has only kept an individual in the same position/ circumstance longer, and allowed a situation to progressively get worst. Your choice is to go back to sleep or to move, but just understand that there will be a direct impact/ influence on not only your life, but also on the lives of your family, friends, and those who are around you. Therefore, ARISE!

The ***sixth critical point*** that is raised is "<u>Sit down!</u>" I am a big fan of this critical point, and here's why. This point in conjunction with the previous point says, "Arise, and Sit down!" Although these commands seem to contradict themselves, they are extremely enlightening as it relates to our moving forward. Here's how: When we are told to get up (arise), then sit back down, it doesn't command as an approach or an intent for us to sit back down in our same posture, the same position, or even the same place. Rather, this speaks to us being able to sit down in a higher place, a place of dignity, a place that will be more suited for someone who has just overcome their circumstance and seeks to lead others to do the same.

We must now get up off the ground and now SIT in a chair, to avoid the dirt and filth that would love to keep us consumed. <u>We get up from our ground-level state where we allowed others to walk all over us</u> *(as stated in the Isaiah 51:22-23)*; we now get up with a new mindset and alert spirit, and we sit in a "successful" place worthy of royalty *(mind, body, and spirit)*. We MUST refuse to sit back down in places that we have allowed to rob us of our dignity, our confidence, our purpose, and of POWER!

The last two verses from Isaiah 51 set up the first two verses that we are reviewing in Isaiah 52. The last two verses in Isaiah 51 say:

Isaiah 51:22-23 Vs. 22 *"Thus saith thy Lord the Lord, and thy God that pleadeth the cause of his* *people, Behold, I have taken out of thine hand the cup of trembling, even the dregs of the cup of my fury; thou shalt no more drink it again:"* **Vs. 23** *"But I will put it into the hand of them that afflict thee; which have said to thy soul, Bow down, that we may go over:* **and thou hast laid thy body as the ground, and as the street, to them that went over**."

Get up off the ground! Stop letting people walk all over you! Stop accepting that just because you have been knocked down in life, you can't get back up and live! Take your opportunity to prove them wrong, namely all of those who don't really know who you are. These are folks who only know what they've seen while you were on the "dock," or while you were in the "pig pen," or while you were lying on the ground scared to move, letting them walk over you. Tell somebody, "I GET IT NOW! I **GET** *(understand)* what I **GOT** *(what I have)*!"

The ***seventh critical point*** that is raised is "Loose thyself from the bands of thy neck!"

As I mentioned before, this text speaks to the children of Israel coming out of captivity and becoming free of their bondage. And what was true then is true now for those who have found themselves in captivity due to their own actions. This seventh critical point says the most profound thing you will hear in this chapter. It says that we must loose ourselves from the bands around our necks (period/ full stop). That is to say, from the things that we are allowing to hold us back from making progress, and moving forward in getting (obtaining) what we want by getting (understanding) what we got (what we already have). What has been given to us is the power to "loose" ourselves from our own baggage and circumstances which have consistently hindered our progress and success in life. See, no one can put baggage in your hands unless first you are willing to accept it from them.

In short, when you are the cause of your chains; then God says in Isaiah 52, that you must be the one to free yourself. Yes, God gives you the power to do it, ABSOLUTELY, but **make NO mistake**, *you* **are** solely responsible for executing that power. Which leads me to say this: If you were willing to walk into the pig pen, then you yourself must be willing to walk out of it in order for you to be free. Crazy, I know, because we like to demand of the Lord that He get us out of our trouble. Yet we are not truly understanding (or getting) that the talents, gifts, purpose, and POWER that He has already given to us allows us to both get up and to get out of our circumstances.

The second most important insight to this power is not that it can get us up, or even out of our bondage, but that it has the ability to also help us to avoid getting there in the first place. Of course, the first most important insight is that once we have moved and made progress, then we are obligated to help others in the same manner so they can do the same.

If you don't remember anything else from this, just remember that I'm not the one telling you to LOOSE YOURSELF, God Himself said this command directly to you. So on this last critical point, I want to say that we are given an understanding that we must let go of those "chains" that have been holding us back and keeping us from "getting what we want" (the desires of our heart). This is the last step in this process, to unlock, to break, to discard, to loose those "bands" that we have around our neck. And whatever you do, don't let them keep choking the life out you and forcing you to stay in bondage. Some of us allow our past failures to be our "bands," some allow past relationships to hold us back, some allow what people have said about us to be the baggage that holds us back from living, but **WHATEVER** "it" is, we must…

Awake, awake,

Put on our strength,

Put on our best appearance, or version of ourselves,

Shake the dust off of us,

GET UP out of that pig pen,

Sit down in a better place, a place more suitable for someone like

yourself who is in pursuit of your purpose,

And then release yourself from whatever has been holding you

back. In short, **DON'T PACK, JUST *MOVE*!!!**

Now I know this information is challenging for many of us to

swallow and digest, if for no other reason than it's just not what we have

been taught. We have been taught that God's role in our success is all that

is needed. However, what you've been reading, and what you are about to

read in this next few chapters, will reshape some of your theology,

Christology, and even some of your practical thinking. That said, grab

some tea, some coffee, or something good to drink, and go with me to the

next chapter. I think this one will have you even more intrigued, and

energized about moving forward.

CHAPTER THREE

"Why is there lack in the Church?"

Keeping in the context of this book, this chapter will prove to be very informative and will take necessary steps to keep us moving forward. The title is simple, but to understand it in its totality will take some of us out of our comfort zone. See, what we are going to discuss in this chapter is how too many of us are looking for "things" in this life: a Porsche, a Ferrari, a yacht, a private jet, a good job, a successful business, etc. And though all of these things may be fun to have, these should not be an obsession, motive, or the focus for our lives. These things are only byproducts of what our purpose can produce.

Helping each other to achieve greatness is a mutual purpose that we all share, and when we both succeed, we can all enjoy the best this life has to offer. Of course, we have to want to succeed, which means we have to allow ourselves to be taught, to apply ourselves to study, and to both grow and move. This is the mindset: When I do better, my family does better; but when you and I both do better, our community does better, and so forth.

Now, as a Christian I believe that the church has a vital role in the establishing and maturing of an individual's understanding of God, and also as being the beacon in the community. In fact, since church buildings have been erected, even up until as late as the late 1800's, most places in the world restricted the height of buildings to be shorter than the church.

Thus, the church could be seen as the prominent institution in the community. However, in today's society, the church is dwarfed in its importance both physically and in its influence in the community. It is dwarfed physically by big banks that typically own the skyline in just about every major city across the world. And the church is also dwarfed in its influence in most communities because of what the very same banks represent.

In today's modern church, we often find these two conflicting points—obtaining "things" and the role of the church—have become blurred. Some church leaders will say that they believe we can enjoy nice things, but what they mean is that "they" can enjoy nice things and we (the congregation) can help financially support the mission. If they meant all of us, then they would slow down their enjoyment of the "things" until they had at least equipped the people with the understanding of how to be equally successful. This "equipping" is experienced in spirituality as well as practicality.

Church leadership should not just teach on the blood of goats and bullocks in the bible, or on the laws of Moses, but should teach on the blood of Jesus, and on the practical use of the bible in this day in age. What am I saying? I'm saying that the church needs to stop "surface teaching/preaching" and get into the depth of the word of God so the people can be equally elevated and freed from religion and tradition.

Listen, I have no problem with church leaders having a $65MM jet, a

Rolls Royce, big houses, etc. That is to say, I don't have a problem with

this **<u>AS LONG AS</u>** they are not simply preaching "God wants you to

have…", and are actually educating, **AND** supporting their parishioners on

how to obtain the same. All things that pertain to <u>life</u> **AND** <u>Godliness</u>

should be taught to the people of God.

> **2 Peter 1:3** *<u>According as his divine power hath</u>*
>
> *<u>given unto us all things that pertain unto life and</u>*
>
> *<u>godliness, through the knowledge of him that hath</u>*
>
> *<u>called us to glory and virtue:</u>*" (KJV)

My only point here is that church leaders should not have what

their congregations do not have, <u>unless</u> the church leaders themselves

happen to have personally bought and own these items outright. That is,

without using church funds, church tax ID, or anything other than his/her

salary. This should, by the way, be reasonable (period/ full stop). They

should not have these things hidden under the banner of the church in

order to avoid taxes and enjoy nonprofit living while the congregation

pays taxes, AND is giving of the tithes & offerings that make these

"things" available.

Now of course, the whole congregation doesn't have to have these kinds of items/things, because we already know that a percentage of them simply won't apply what is taught, and others will lack the needed discipline required to obtain these things, but for those that do seek to enjoy the fruits of their labor, they should be given the necessary knowledge to do so. The key for us to grasp here is not so much in having these things, but rather in obtaining the knowledge that gives access to the things. See, with knowledge you can get access to things, but things don't necessarily give you access to knowledge.

<Commercial Break…>

Let me make one additional point extremely clear: If you are a church leader and you are enjoying a private jet, expensive cars, big houses, etc., then do so at your own expense. If not, and if these items belong to the church, then keep in mind that the church should have access to them as well. If the church Usher President, Singles Ministry President, or Outreach Minister, Youth group, etc. has a conference to attend, then shouldn't they also have access to the private jet or expensive cars that their tithes/offerings have helped to purchase and/or make payments? Or if a parishioner is foreclosed on, or evicted from their home, shouldn't they have access to the big mansion for a set time? If the church members do not have access to what the church members have paid for and that the church now owns, then there is something unmistakably wrong with how the church is being led.

<*...and we're back*>

Now, let's slow this down a bit and look at this from a different perspective, and then work our way back to where we started in the intro of this chapter. And as we do so, we will get a more lucid comprehension of *"Why is there lack in the Church?"*

What we have been taught to do since we were children is to listen to our parents, study hard, get good grades, and have fun. This is all good stuff, worthy to be taught and good for a child to understand, we would all agree. And once that child gets of a certain age, we then explain to that child that he or she will now need to <u>go to college, find a good job, work hard, maybe get married, have some children, and save for retirement</u>. This, too, by the way, is not fundamentally bad to teach our children; the only drawback with this is that these things are all just common, they are normal, and they are ordinary. If this is something you personally want for your life, then there is NO problem, and NO shame in doing so. Now, if you are teaching or mentoring some young person today and doing so from a Godly perspective, then your mindset should have moved from a common to an <u>uncommon</u> approach *(rare, extraordinary, and/or unusual)*.

As those who are in Christ, we are told to be unusual, special, or unique, even unconventional.

1 Peter 2:9-10 Vs. 9 *<u>But ye are a chosen generation, a royal priesthood, an holy nation, a peculiar people</u>; that ye should shew forth the praises of him who hath called you out of darkness into his marvellous light;"* **Vs. 10** *"Which in time past were not a people, but are now the people of God: which had not obtained mercy, but now have obtained mercy."* (KJV)

Now unfortunately, all too often in the church we only get a religious or surface understanding of this scripture and many other scriptures throughout the bible. Therefore, <u>we shout, we sing, we emotionally react to sermons and praise teams</u>, but rarely do we move to a greater understanding of the scripture, our relationship with God, or a better approach to life.

See, we find that most of what is taught in churches concerning "preparation for success" is not much different than what we have been taught from the common approach *(go to college, find a good job, work hard, maybe get married, have some children, and save for retirement).*

Sure, one is practical in its performance and the other is religious in its performance. One is systematic in its approach to mediocrity, and the other motivates our emotions to simply rejoice in mediocrity. We know that life is not to be lived completely conservative or without a "leap of faith." We know that we have to jump into the pool with both feet if we want to have our whole body immersed.

Having a spiritual relationship with God is vastly different from religion. A spiritual relationship at its core is like any physical relationship, it requires both give and take. A relationship cannot be one-sided, because after all, who wants to be in a relationship where there is no participation from the other party? Selah! We'll get into this in more detail in a minute, but first let's talk about…

What is the church today teaching?

There are a lot of churches today that preach prosperity-laced messages. They teach that God wants you to be rich in finances, and that God wants us to have private jets and mega mansions as rewards for our giving. The church today has become a hype squad or pep rally, only motivating us to give money, volunteer time, and be gathered together to pray, sing, dance, and salute the leaders for facilitating the work. Now, I'm not saying that all of those things are wrong, but like anything else they have to be considered in context. If these are the only things that we are doing in church, then we are failing our purpose. The church is to equip the saints through the word of God on who God is, what He has done through Christ, and who He created us to be. It is also to equip us on how we should live in helping others, and what God has made available to us, both in this life and the next life. There should be education in both spiritual and practical matters of life. We can't just say to the people "give" and not equip the people with the understanding on how to obtain something to give; we can't just say "give more," but not equip the people with the understanding on how to obtain more.

I'll say it this way: If someone gives you a cow, you should at least give them some cheese. This simply means that if God, through the church, is freely giving you the understanding of how to create wealth and how to help people with the wealth, then you should be willing to freely give back to God through that particular church, wouldn't you agree? However, this takes work, and the cycle begins with the House of God or what we commonly call "the church". And yes, this should be holistic in spiritual growth, wealth, health, social living, and more. Then this becomes a mutual relationship that continues to reproduce and regenerate itself over and over again. In other words, we begin to be fruitful and multiply (Genesis 1:28).

It's been often said that "you can't get blood from a turnip," which simply means that you can't get money from someone that doesn't have it to give. In so many churches today, this is the well-defined approach and playbook for raising money for everything in the church *(from a new roof, to a new building, to a new private jet, to Pastor's appreciation, etc.)* Therefore, to keep up with the demand and with additional projects, church leaders steer their focus toward increasing church membership instead of increasing discipleship. Of course, 'more people/ more money' is a pretty basic principle, yet it's still a calculated and slothful method of obtaining new revenue. Consequently, I believe that there are three main reasons why this approach is flawed:

1. The obvious reason for this approach being flawed is because church membership should never be a focus to begin with; the focus should at all times be on discipleship.

   - If you make it about church membership (revenue/ money), then you undoubtedly make this transactional, and then in turn set your Godly relationship as a membership to a church and not as a member of the body of Christ more specifically.

   - If you make it about revenue, that constitutes a "membership." Then simple logic would say that if you educate your congregation with practical teaching on how to increase personal wealth, then they would become more financially free. And if they become more financially free, then they will have more available finances. And if they have more available finances, then they can give more financial support to the work of Christ via the church. Look, its simple mathematics and a simple business principle. Would you want to be a manager of 1,500 members bringing in $8MM in annual revenue, or have 150 members with $8MM in annual revenue? Of course, you'd choose the latter; it's less overhead (from the perspective of the building size needed), less oversight (the number of people), which gives you the ability to focus more time/money into the community. This allows more attention on the parishioners so that they can mature in the faith, and God can send them out to help more folks in need, thus organically growing the church versus launching a pseudo marketing campaign to increase church membership.

2. The second reason this is a flawed approach is that it's just the laziest method for raising money. This takes absolutely no real effort from the leaders to collect money from others, or ask them to bring a friend or family member to church with them. In fact, the leader doesn't even have to do the collecting, or even count the money, just instruct the congregation to give. That said, you can see that this approach offers little to nothing to those who are doing the giving, while some leaders simultaneously request more money for doing so.

3. This last reason is actually a summation of the first two. While He was on the earth, Christ gave of Himself to meet the needs of the people. And then He commissioned us (His Church) to continue to meet the needs of the people until His return. Therefore, if this is not being done in the church today, then the church is not fulfilling its purpose and it is ultimately flawed.

From a practical standpoint, the church does not teach how to obtain finances. Church leaders just typically say, "It's giving time!", and most parishioners are then guilted into giving. Or they say to their parishioners other things such as "The more you give, the more you get;" I don't have a particular challenge with this, <u>OTHER THAN</u> this only tends to describe the latter part of the financial process. See, giving only comes about **AFTER** you have obtained something to give. *AMEN SOMEBODY!!!*

The challenge that I often find in the church is that we habitually make it a priority to teach on the "what" to give *(money)*, and the "how" to give *(cheerfully)*. Yet too often, we lack the practical teaching on how to obtain "something" in order to have "something" more to give. And sadly, the fact is that if some church leaders can't properly manage the church money, or support their congregants on how to increase their personal revenue flow, then how ridiculous and insulting is it for leaders to ask congregants for more money, Selah! Many church leaders don't know how to "create" wealth, they only know how to "take" wealth.

We are created in the image and likeness of God and He is The Creator; therefore, man has creative abilities that are intended to be used for the greater good of all. Creative ability, in this sense, simply means that we should conceive multiple streams of wealth and programs to help others. We will look at and talk about this more in depth in the next chapters. In the meantime…

Let's continue this chapter by working our way through scripture and see a systematic approach to how the church should meet the needs of the people. It makes sense for us to look at this from the perspective of the "people," and then once we understand what it is the people need, we can then easily conclude what the church should be teaching and providing. Make sense? Good!

Since there are so many of you reading this book at different levels of spiritual understanding, let's start from the beginning to hopefully bring more clarity. First…

> **Genesis 2:7** *"And **the Lord God formed man of the dust of the ground**, and breathed into his nostrils the breath of life; and man became a living soul."*
> (KJV)

Here's the first thing to recognize: We would be nothing but dust if it had not been for God breathing life into us; this should help keep us humbled and grounded as we take this journey. Secondly, we should recognize that God does everything in order; thus, before He took the action to breathe life into the dust (us), He had to first make the dust. Let that one sink in for a moment!

Now for some who like to get even more granular, I can hear your question, "How do we know that God made the dust; how do we know that to be true?" Well, because…

John 1:1-4 Vs. 1 *"In the beginning was the Word, and the Word was with God, and the Word was God."* **Vs. 2** *"The same was in the beginning with God."* **Vs. 3** *"**All things were made by him; and without him was not any thing made that was made**."* **Vs. 4** *"In him was life; and the life was the light of men."* (KJV)

Therefore, this part becomes a super critical point. As a matter of fact, this gives a very clear account of **how** we came to be. However, seeing that this is not enough, we need to also understand and accept **why** we came to be…

Ephesians 2:8-10 Vs. 8 *"For by grace are ye saved through faith; and that not of yourselves: it is the gift of God:"* **Vs. 9** *"Not of works, lest any man should boast."* **Vs. 10** *"**For we are his workmanship, created in Christ Jesus unto good works**, which God hath before ordained that we should walk in them."* (KJV)

Now stay with me, because this is where some of you may start seeing things a little differently for the first time. We've just read that it's

God who created us for good works, and therefore, it's God who gives us the power (breath of life) to perform those works. After all, it was God who created the dust and used it to form able bodies to perform the works. This sovereign approach to creation and purpose actually prevents us from **taking** credit, as if we did these works all ourselves. Nonetheless, with that being said, I do believe that we are **given** some credit by God. See, **taking** credit implies that either it belongs to us in the first place, or we are going to steal it from someone else. Oppositely, **giving** credit implies that we humbly turn something we own over to another person or persons. In the case of God, we give to Him a portion of that which He has already given to us, seeing that all things come from Him in the first place.

It should not be a surprise that God gives us credit/a pat on the back for the things that He has given us to do. It should equally not be surprising that God allows us to be rewarded for our obedience to do those things.

God gives us all a choice to accept or not accept His word, to move or not to move based on what He has spoken in His word (this moving is both spiritual and often natural). A good illustration of this is the story of the man at the pool of Bethesda that we read about in chapter one, when Jesus said to him, *"Rise, take up thy bed, and walk!"* Simply put, there are things that he needed to do, and yes, ultimately it was done through God's power which God imparted to the man. Nonetheless, the man had to, just as any of us would have to, make a conscious choice to accept and to use both the power and the opportunities given by God.

Therefore, there is still credit <u>given</u> to those who take action on God's word, albeit very minuscule in comparison to what God has already done to make these works available, but credit nonetheless. That said, it is highly important that you don't miss the point that I'm making, which is that God has made it possible for us to "do" (period/ full stop). And then when we "do," He gives us a little credit/ pat on the back for applying His power, and for taking full advantage of the opportunity that He has presented to us. If you are reading this and you are a parent this may make even more sense to you. Let's also take a look at the scripture below to further this point of having credit/ a pat on the back…

> **Matthew 25:21** *"**His lord said unto him, Well done**, thou good and faithful servant: **thou hast been faithful over a few things, I will make thee ruler over many things**: enter thou into the joy of thy lord."* (KJV)

Yes, God <u>gives</u> credit/ a pat on the back if you work His principles (period/ full stop). And as I mentioned above I will be expounding on this more, and even to a greater extent in chapter four using a more appropriate

scripture focus text.

Now let's pivot slightly and highlight some of these "good works"

which are all about helping others, feeding the hungry, giving those who

are thirsty something to drink, giving clothes to those who are in need.

And in addition to those good works we have: lending a helping hand to

strangers, going to hospitals and treatment centers to visit with the sick,

and visiting those in who are incarcerated. Incidentally, these visits to

hospitals, prisons, etc., are not about us just showing up, but should

include sharing of the gospel, teaching practical life lessons, and giving

encouragement to others to accept their God-given "overcoming" ability

to move forward.

These things holistically change lives, and influence/impact lives

in communities across the world to the extent that you may never fully be

aware of or understand. While I'm on this point, let me add this: works are

both equally individual, as well as corporately obligatory. In other words,

we each have works to do both individually, and corporately together, and

we are obligated to do so. This is important if you are looking to get a full

understanding of this teaching, because too many of us, especially in the

church, only believe in the corporate works. This is typically because most prefer to hide in the crowd and not contribute 100% of their part. They prefer to simply sit back and look at everyone else and say, "well they got this!" or "they can handle this, they don't need me."

There are also those who are considered to be just sittin' on the dock of the bay **<u>wastin' time</u>**." They say things like, *"Well, I'm just a humble servant of God, so I work behind the scenes."* What in the world does *"...I work behind the scenes"* even mean exactly? If this is in reference to some sort of humility, then yes, we can agree that the bible does teach humility…

> **Romans 12:3** *<u>"For I say, through the grace given unto me, to every man that is among you,</u> **<u>not to think of himself more highly than he ought to think</u>**<u>; but to think soberly, according as God hath dealt to every man the measure of faith."</u>* (KJV)

> **Proverbs 16:18-19 Vs. 18** *<u>"Pride goeth before destruction, and an haughty spirit before a fall."</u>*
> **Vs. 19** *<u>"Better it is to be of an humble spirit with the lowly, than to divide the spoil with the proud."</u>* (KJV)

And yet, though the bible clearly teaches humility, it **<u>DOES NOT</u>** teach that we are to be *"…behind the scenes,"* or in some sort of background position. In fact, the word of God actually declares and makes clear the exact opposite…

> **Matthew 5:14-16** Vs. 14 <u>*Ye are the light of the world. A city that is set on an hill cannot be hid*</u>*."* **Vs. 15** *"*<u>**Neither do men light a candle, and put it under a bushel**</u><u>*, but on a candlestick; and it giveth light unto all that are in the house.*</u>*"* **Vs. 16** *"*<u>**Let your light so shine before men, that they may see your good works, and glorify your Father which is in heaven**</u>*."* (KJV)

> **Deuteronomy 28:13 Vs. 13** *"*<u>**And the Lord shall make thee the head, and not the tail; and thou shalt be above only, and thou shalt not be beneath**</u><u>*; if that thou hearken unto the commandments of the Lord thy God, which I command thee this day, to observe and to do them:*</u>*"* (KJV)

Certainly, we are meant to be out front, to be examples of how to move from the bottom of life to the top, while helping others to do precisely the same. We're meant to be following God, growing spiritually, and financially so as to make a powerful impact in this life and leave a mark. And though giving money is a small thing, it is still a required thing for those who obtain it, and have it to give…

Luke 12:48 *"But he that knew not, and did commit things worthy of stripes, shall be beaten with few stripes.* ***For unto whomsoever much is given, of him shall be much required: and to whom men have committed much, of him they will ask the more.*** *"* (KJV)

And of course, this scripture is not about money only, and does include all things that have been given, yet money is certainly coherent in this text. And while on this point, it's important that we have been given the power to obtain finances, so we can use it to aid us in fulfilling our purpose, to help us better grasp what we have been provided let's remember a scripture from chapter two…

Deuteronomy 8:18 *"But thou shalt remember the Lord thy God:* ***for it is he that giveth thee power to get wealth,*** *that he may establish his covenant* *which he sware unto thy fathers, as it is this day."*

KJV

Yes, God lets us know that it is **He** who has given us power to get wealth.

Wealth is something that God intended for us, and it is something that **NONE OF US** should be ashamed of having in this life. Let me say it again, **NONE OF US** should be ashamed of what we have in this life. According to the passage of scripture we just looked at, God gave us the "power" to get "wealth," but He did not simply hand us the "wealth." I need to be clear on that. I've quoted this a thousand times and I'll quote it again, "Faith without works is dead." Therefore, we have to accept the power, understand the power, and apply/ work the power to get what God says we can "get." And if God gave the power to us, then it must be good for us to have, and for all those who we help through the process.

Understand that it takes a seed to bring about a harvest, and even God gave a seed in His Son Jesus The Christ so that He may bring about many brethren. So it is with wealth. If you are inclined to ask for it, God doesn't always give it to you in the form of a miracle, though He can and He does at times. Rather, generally speaking, God will give a "seed," the business idea, the person to help, the movie/ song/ play/ or even the book to write. You asked for a million dollars and God says, "Okay, here is the power *(idea & belief)* that you will need to obtain the harvest *(the millions)."*

There are really ONLY two reasons we don't have more success in life: Either 1) we don't understand what to do with the seed, or 2) we don't understand what to do with the harvest. We don't work our seed so we fail our harvest, or to be more pointed, if we don't work our moment, then we are failing our future. The seed is synonymous with the moment; get the seed, then you are in your moment. I hope this is helping someone understand that we need more teaching in the church!!

Now then, as I stated before *"giving only comes about **AFTER** you have obtained something to give."* And *"Yet too often we lack the practical teaching on how to obtain "something" in order to have "something" to give."* Keep in mind, the more you get, and/or have, the more you have to give. This is not a challenging statement. It doesn't take a college degree or a doctorate in theological studies. In truth, any child, let alone an adult, could understand this concept. We can all help someone regardless of where you are in life, either financially, or by teaching through understanding/ experience, or both. There is always someone doing worse than you, someone trying to get where you are, someone trying to unpack decades of baggage to move to the street that you are living on right now. And though you may not have thousands of dollars to help them now, you at the very minimum have the knowhow to share with them how you got there, and that *(as we just read about a second ago)* you are required to share.

Now, the goal of this portion of the chapter is to elaborate on what I strongly believe the church should be doing. This brings us back full circle to the intro of this chapter. The church/ church leadership should broaden its perspective on how to obtain finances within the church. Too often the church is way too small-minded and on autopilot with its thirst for receiving money, and not strategic enough in its ability to be fruitful and multiply *(a reference to my previous book, "Be Fruitful and Multiply")*.

The last book spoke to the holistic meaning to "be fruitful and multiply" in a way that informs us that God intends for us to have multiple births, multiple streams of "success." That is to say simply success in every area of life. The church of late has been reduced to one stream of revenue, and that is directly through the pockets of its congregants. Of course, this is not in every church, and granted the congregants should be giving, but church leaders have to be wiser than this and be able to absorb what God is saying.

2 Corinthians 9:6 *"<u>But this I say, **He which**</u>*

*<u>**soweth sparingly shall reap also sparingly; and he**</u>*

*<u>**which soweth bountifully shall reap also**</u>*

*<u>**bountifully**</u>."* (KJV)

The church of late has been more performance based rather than teaching, more running guilt trips rather than leading by example. When is the last time the church, in general, sowed into the life of its congregation?? I'm not talking about what you've done for those in other countries, or those in other major cities; I'm asking about within your church. I'm not talking about keeping the lights on in the church, or having the marble floors polished and having the air and water running, etc. I'm talking about sowing as it is preached in pulpits all across the country. Sowing meaning "above" the obligated portion. See, taking care of the utilities and upkeep of the church facility is not "above"; those things are just the standard obligations. This is the equivalent of congregants' personal giving when told to go above their standard obligations.

Let me help someone…when is the last time that you laid eyes on someone who walked down to the altar *(not asking for anything)* and the church offered to bless this person by paying their monthly mortgage bill? Or when is the last time you saw church leaders call out parishioners in service to give them other types of monetary assistance, or to offer to send them on trip to get away from some of the stress in his/her life? We have to lead by example! We can't keep telling the saints/ congregants to perform these types of $100, $1000, $5000 giving actions to help the church and/or others in need if the church is not willing to be the optical example of what they desire to see in the people. Again, this is **NOT** all churches; there are a lot of churches that are doing a fantastic job at assisting their members both openly and privately, formally and informally *(spontaneously)*. They have supportive programs and education that helps their parishioners to metaphorically drop their baggage and move forward in life. Nonetheless, there are plenty of churches that are simply religious performers, having seemingly no relationship with God, or with the people of God.

There are church leaders who will verbally beat up their parishioners for not giving more to help support the church's "special projects." And yet some of these parishioners are guilted into giving both their seed *and* their harvest to the church, and then still are asked for more *(now that's a book all in itself)*. Some church leaders will guilt congregants during Christmas season for maxing out credit cards and living above their means, yet the underlying concern is not the congregants at all; it's their decreased financial giving to the church during that time of the year.

Conversely, some church leaders are doing the exact same things as it relates to the church's money. They're irresponsible, building a bigger church with no growth in their congregation. They are putting on expensive concerts and "religious" conferences, all with money they don't currently have and simply call it acting on faith. And instead of scaling back their "special projects," they just ask for more money from the attendees at their churches. Isn't this the same thing that these same leaders are preaching against when it comes to the personal finances of their congregants??? Don't max out credit cards, because it means that you are spending more than what you have, it's the same both personally and as it relates to the church. It's the same thing; the message is about us being more responsible.

I'm going to say it again, how can the church expect money to be given if you don't first teach on how to get money?? Take this analogy: If your child is given a test at school and the teacher never taught the subject that the test is on, then how can the child be expected to pass the test? And as a parent, when you find out the circumstances of why your child failed the test, you will be at the school letting everyone know your displeasure. So it is on this subject. How does the church expect people to give if they have not been taught first on how to get? Remember chapter two, to **GET** *(to obtain)* what you want you have to **GET** *(having understanding)* of what you **GOT** *(what you already have)*. If you don't "have," you can't "get." Say amen somebody! Let me say it another way, and in such a way that the world would understand: "It *takes* money to *make* money."

Now you may say this suggests or puts a lot on the church to do, and my response would be, yes you're right, but *I'm* not putting it on the church, *God* is. God says that the church is responsible and thus will be judged first. Not the President, not the Governor, not the Mayor, not the local officials, or the schools. The leaders of these entities all certainly have their part to play in helping others, and they will answer for their actions, but as God says…

> **1 Peter 4:17** *"For the time is come that **judgment must begin at the house of God**: and if it first begin at us, what shall the end be of them that obey not the gospel of God?"* (KJV)

The church has a responsibility to be a place where believers can learn everything to advance their life, because everything is relevant to God. See, having good health in life is just as important as having meaningful relationships, and just as important as having good stewardship over your finances. In this earthly life, there is one thing we all, believer and nonbelievers, have in common, and that is that money is necessary. It is not the most preeminent; that spot is reserved for God and it is His alone, yet money is unequivocally necessary. One of the wisest men to ever walk the earth *(having Godly wisdom)* said…

Ecclesiastes 10:19 *"A feast is made for laughter, and wine maketh merry: **but money answereth all things**."* (KJV)

Another translation says: *"…But it's money that makes the world go around."* (MSG)

So, what should the church do?

The church **HAS TO** be a place where people can learn how to get ahead both spiritually and practically. This certainly starts and ends with the teaching of Christ. And through that teaching, there should be some practical teachings that are freely given to those congregants of the church, such as, but not limited to:

- Personal finance training   /   Resume writing classes

- Mock interview training   /   Computer & Digital training

- Job placement programs   /   Church business directory *(creating revenue)*

- How to invest money (real estate, 401k, IRA's, etc.)

- Basic Business classes (How to start a business, how to purchase a business, etc.)

- And of course, there are a lot of other practical things like how to live healthy on a budget, marriage counseling, family counseling (living with, or in, a blended household, etc.), how to cope with stress, and more. These are all equally critical things that need to be discussed and outlined for God's people to be successful.

What's funny is that churches have educational training for other practical things, such as a lot of the things we just mentioned *(health, marriages, parenting, and more)*. However, it's interesting that the church lacks teaching in the area of financial literacy, which is why there seems to be so much lack in the church. And it's interesting because finances are one of the main means by which we support the church, and are a lot of the initiatives we seek to obtain success, both for ourselves and for helping others.

How many in the church are living paycheck to paycheck and yet are saying "I love my church; I've been a member for 30 years." Wait, what?? Loving your church is a great thing, and I would suggest if you don't love it, that's a good sign for you to leave. You will probably just become disruptive and hateful eventually, which will not edify or help anyone, so just go about your business. The church should have your financial support, your time, and talent to edify the members and the community. Yet my challenge is the fact that you have been at your church for 30 years and are still living paycheck to paycheck, which means that **A)** you haven't learned anything that the leadership had been teaching you and it's your fault, or **B)** the leadership has failed you by not providing you with the understanding that you need in order to be successful and impactful in this life. Either way, 30 years in this case is not a badge of honor.

When the congregation and community see how the church is building businesses and developing other methods of revenue, it will encourage them that this can be done on a personal level as well. I have seen a lot of church leaders who have expanded the wealth of the church and of the people of the church to do some amazing things in their communities. One example is a church in Baltimore, Maryland, that had started a car service business with a sedan and then later purchased multiple cars to include limousines. This same church bought vacant buildings around the neighborhood and turned those into training centers and addiction centers and receives monies from other organizations for support. There are churches that own thrift stores, and bookstores that are generating additional income for their outreach programs and building expansion programs for more classrooms. This is what must happen in the church so that not only is the gospel supported, but it's supported in a way that makes the words of the gospel come alive for those in need. The church can give more **WITHOUT** being a burden to the people who are seeking the teaching that will give them guidance and direction to a better life.

When the church adopts this mentality to do this type of creative way of receiving and giving, then the church will see a change in what is being given back. See, we lead by example; therefore, in some cases, as the church goes, so go the people. If the church is financially illiterate, then there should be NO surprise that the people whom they are to edify would also be financially illiterate. Not all of the people of course, because some come to the church with prior financial knowledge, etc. However, if a church leader does not know how to create multiple streams of income in order to help more people, then they should not have an unreal expectation of the congregation doing it. Again, as a church leader you have to lead by example and position the church to have other streams of income so as to not tax the congregation with personally supporting every initiative of the church. The church should own businesses to help absorb some of the church cost, while simultaneously supporting the communities with goods and services.

> **John 21:15-17** *"He saith unto him the third time, Simon, son of Jonas, lovest thou me? Peter was grieved because he said unto him the third time, Lovest thou me? And he said unto him, Lord, thou knowest all things; thou knowest that I love thee.* ***Jesus saith unto him, Feed my sheep****."* (KJV)

As I mentioned, some business ideas for churches can include a rental hall, t-shirts, bookstore, car services, and many other things. The church should use wisdom and become more creative and more resourceful in generating revenue to better edify the people of God and the communities in which they have been geographically assigned.

> **Matthew 10:16** *"Behold, I send you forth as sheep in the midst of wolves:* ***be ye therefore wise as serpents, and harmless as doves****."* (KJV)

Being creative, clever, and resourceful is what God has equipped us with and called us to do in order to perform good works. Each of us has to avoid packing those old religious ways of doing things, to include our church leaders, and we have to take a leap of faith and make the decision to MOVE! For some, the first step of our move is to find another church that can better support who we are, once we better realize who we are called to be. UNCOMMON!!

Say this, ***"I AM NOT A PEW WARMER!"***

Say, ***"I AM GREATER THAN WHAT OTHERS HAVE TOLD ME!"***

Say, ***"I AM NOT HERE TO SUPPORT YOUR AGENDA, I'M HERE FOR KINGDOM BUSINESS!"***

One of the overall objective of this chapter is to first exhort church leaders to stop putting all the pressure on the congregation for its only source of revenue. Secondly, I'm saying to the congregation to stop enabling lazy leaders and allowing this type of purposeless religion to continue.

As I close this chapter, the church should now know if it did not before, that it can't get blood from a turnip. And equally, it should also now be clear that the church should support its congregation with essential teaching(s) to grow those who are in need, AND it should be creative in its vision to generate new revenue, so as to help others in the church, those in the community, those in the nation, and those throughout the world. And for these essential teachings *(spiritually, and practically),* I believe the congregation should not be financially charged to participate and get the necessary information. At least not on the first time they take the course, if they are coming back a second, and third time then they are taking seats away from others who have not had the teaching at which time each church can determine if it makes sense to charge some sort of "re-entry fee".

Now for those seeking to participate in a local body of believers, here is something to think about. *If you notice that there is a lack in a particular church,* then before deciding to affiliate yourself, you may want to consider a few things:

1. Is the church living above its own means and expecting a stagnant number of congregants to subsidize the poor decisions of leadership?

2. Is it buying a bigger church before there is a need?

3. Is it giving more to the Pastor than to the needs of the people or to the upkeep of the church?

If the church can't manage the money that they are currently getting prior to you getting there, then chances are they won't start with your money.

So likely this is not good ground to sow in and could be a warning sign (*__Matthew 13:3-9__*).

4. Does the church have multiple streams of income; is it practicing what it is teaching?

5. Is the Pastor financially living like the congregation that he, or she is leading? *(Of course you have to take into consideration what that Pastor had prior to becoming the leader of that church, or if he/she has gained simply because they have worked the principles that they are teaching).* If the Pastor is prosperous, is the church?

6. Is the Pastor's anniversary/ appreciation the biggest church event of the year?

   - Nothing wrong with celebrating your Pastor, as a matter of fact I'm a big fan of showing appreciation for those who help us get "off our docks". However, I'm not a fan of anyone wasting time, or money that could otherwise be spent learning, or helping others.

7. If you are gifted in good financial stewardship, then perhaps God led you to this particular church so that your gift can be used to edify God's people.

8. You may also consider that where you are may not be the right church for you to be a part of, and you will likely need to do some additional praying on this one.

9. You should also consider that if this is a place that is properly equipping you for success and you are not willing to properly give back, then this is likely not a place for you to be. You have to support those who support you (period/ full stop).

10. And saving the best for last, is the church teaching Christ Jesus as the means to everything that pertains to life and Godliness, in this life, and the one to come.

Remember we are called to be "uncommon," to be different, to lead, and thus we must work what you heard God say. WE MUST hear it, WE MUST accept/ believe it, WE MUST participate in its preordained victory, and WE MUST allow ourselves to unpack our old ways of thinking and responding, and be willing to ***MOVE FORWARD!!!***

CHAPTER FOUR

"What God did, and What we must do."

Coming off the heels of three great chapters of information, **1)** *"Stop sitting on the dock of the bay ...wasting time,"* **2)** *"To Get what you want, you have to Get what you **Got,***" **3)** *"Why is there lack in the Church?"* I thought it would be necessary to follow-up with the information in this chapter, *"What God did, and What we must do."*

So, without wasting time, let's just dive into this chapter and begin by understanding the title. *"What God did, and what we must do"* in and of itself hints of a precedent that many, Christians and non-Christians alike, understand and have likely benefited from. I'm going to break down the full title in a bit, but let me focus on the latter part of the title first, which says, **"...What we must do."** This portion of the title purely speaks to us being responsible to do something, to participate in our own success. Seeing that we live in a dispensation of time where so many in society feel entitled to just "have" without the desire to do any work, this becomes an important point to remedy. So, let's just go straight for the jugular on this one by using this next text as our opening scripture reference.

> **2 Thessalonians 3:10** *"For even when we were with you, this we commanded you, that **if any would not work, neither should he eat***." (KJV)

This precedent, guideline, or principle merely says to everyone (capable) that if you don't participate in life at some level, then you shouldn't expect to benefit. To put this passage into its full context, take a moment to read, at minimum, 2 Thessalonians 3:6-15. When reading this, we should immediately take note that this principle was not something that was just done to be cruel. In fact, the Apostle Paul gave this command in the name of Jesus to those he was ministering to in Thessalonica, because there were people there who had rejected the idea of working altogether. They were lazy and just seeking to take advantage of those who were working, and to be leeches off their harvest and success. Paul told those whom he had been ministering to *(paraphrasing)*, "don't let these lazy freeloaders live off of you, that's not what I've been teaching. When I was with you, I worked with my own hands to set a good example for you, not to be a "weight" dragging you down and keeping you from moving in victory."

Paul's thought on this was that if I myself didn't take from you, then don't let others do it to you. After all, Paul felt that he had more of a right to be helped by those he was teaching, because he was at least giving them lessons on how to live a full life through Christ Jesus. Yet Paul was saying, I myself didn't take advantage of you and I worked and provided for myself to set a good example. He (Paul) says *(again paraphrasing)*,

"I'm hearing that you have forgotten the principle that I taught you, therefore you're letting these lazy people take advantage of you, and this can no longer be acceptable. I'm telling them now to get to work, stop being busybodies and interfering, and distracting others from their duties, their purpose, and their destinies. Stop being lazy; you are a hindrance to those who are seeking to move forward." Then Paul directs his words toward those who were following his teachings, saying *(paraphrasing again)*, "now even though some of these lazy people shouldn't be allowed to leech off of you, you are however not to count them as enemies. You shouldn't scream or yell at them, you shouldn't kick them out of the town, but you should help them understand that they are pulling everyone down and that their actions do not help anyone." Paul was essentially saying that you should minister to them, but not fellowship with them. And therein is a great word to those in the church today.

There are plenty of people, even in the church, that need to understand better why people are in our lives in this season. Are we to minister to them, or to fellowship with them? Yes it is possible to do both, depending on where you both are in your understanding of God. Ministering means that I am helping you with your need. It is often one-sided in the sense of the effort that is being applied, whereas fellowship is a time when like-minded people come together to build each other up.

102

> **Proverbs 27:17** *"Iron sharpeneth iron; so a man*
>
> *sharpeneth the countenance of his friend."* (KJV)

I see this word as the heart of fellowship. Though this text in

Proverbs speaks to "friends," it is important to note that when the disciples

of Jesus had reached a certain level of understanding, Jesus then

proclaimed them to be "friends." Now, this is not to say that Jesus stopped

ministering to them, because He didn't. This simply means that they had

matured to a point of taking on the knowledge of God.

> **John 15:14-15 Vs. 14** *"**Ye are my friends, if ye do**
>
> ***whatsoever I command you**."* **Vs. 15** *"Henceforth I*
>
> *call you not servants; for the servant knoweth not*
>
> *what his lord doeth: but **I have called you friends;***
>
> *for all things that I have heard of my Father I have*
>
> *made known unto you."* (KJV)

Again, all of what we are talking about is related to 2 Thessalonians 3,

around the 6 - 15 verse, so when possible please read.

Now, I believe that it is required of me to be crystal clear on this

particular point so as to not invalidate this entire project of "Don't Pack,

Just *Move.*" This precedent, this instruction, this command that Paul had

given to these in Thessalonica did not in ANY way, shape, or form, apply to those who may have had a disability. Or to those who may have been too old to physically work, or to infants, or to children too young to be self-dependent through their own works. Paul was speaking to those who were more than capable, who had the ability, the gifting, and the talent, but refused to lift a finger, and instead sought to live off the work of others.

Here's a question based on what we've just discussed: Do you know of or have any lazy people in your life like Paul is describing in 2 Thessalonians 3? And let me say this before you answer…if you say you don't have any like this in your life, then there is a high probability that you are that person in someone else's life. Selah! I believe this to be true, because if you have obtained anything through your work, then there will always be leeches with their hands out trying to take advantage of the fruit of your work. And if you don't have a leech in your life, then you have likely not worked to obtain anything worth taking advantage of, and by not having anything, you yourself by default become the leech! I hope you are following that, because it is an important revelation for some who are reading this right now.

REMINDER Remember what I said in the introduction of the book… *As with a lot of what we are discussing in this book, you will* *typically hear the scriptures exposed in a manner that the church today will often overlook, or simply sugarcoat.*

Why did I say all that and give so much time to this passage of scripture? It was to further highlight the second part of the title of this chapter, which says, ***"…What we must do."*** So, to make this short and extremely clear, YOU MUST BE FOUND WORKING! This is a fundamental harmony with life that each of us **(especially the men)** have to come to grips with, because without this very basic knowledge of work, this book or any other motivational or inspirational books will not help you to move.

Work is synonymous with our belief; you **CANNOT** have one without the other, and this is for the believer as much as it is for the non-believer. This is another principle that works if you apply yourself to it fully.

Listen, God said…

Matthew 5:43-45 Vs. 43 *"Ye have heard that it hath been said, Thou shalt love thy neighbour, and hate thine enemy."* **Vs. 44** *"But I say unto you, Love your enemies, bless them that curse you, do good to them that hate you, and pray for them which* *despitefully use you, and persecute you;"* **Vs. 45**

"That ye may be the children of your Father which is in heaven: **for he maketh his sun to rise on the evil and on the good, and sendeth rain on the just and on the unjust**.*"* (KJV)

The latter part of this passage tells us very plainly that God is no respecter of persons and, therefore, His principles when applied can benefit you regardless of your spirituality. God extends His love to everyone and is just, therefore what we perceive to be good, and what we perceive to be bad happens in each of our lives. However, the main point is that our works and our beliefs *(whatever they may be)* have to be synonymous.

Now, before some of us Christians begin to freak out on that last statement, let me just remind us what the bible says to us in this familiar scripture…

John 3:16 *"**For God so loved the world, that he gave his only begotten Son**, that whosoever believeth in him should not perish, but have everlasting life.*"* (KJV)

He gave His Son for us all; how much more of a leap is it that He allows for the sun and the rain to fall on both the **believer and the non-believer**?

This gives legitimacy to my point that there are Godly principles that work regardless of your beliefs. As a matter of fact, if it wasn't for God's passion for the world, then neither you nor I would be able to call ourselves believers to begin with, based on what we just read in John 3:16. Now I'm **NOT** saying that all are saved. That's a silly argument with no scriptural basis; therefore, it's a completely different topic altogether. All I'm saying is that there are biblical principles that whether applied by a believer or non-believer, would still yield some results.

There is a story in the bible that further articulates what happens when you operate in a principle of God. Like the principle that Paul speaks of, which I like to call "work and eat". Jesus tells the story and says the following:

Luke 16:1-8 Vs. 1 *"And he said also unto his disciples, There was a certain rich man, which had a steward; and the same was accused unto him that he had wasted his goods."* **Vs. 2** *"And he called him, and said unto him, How is it that I hear this of thee? give an account of thy stewardship; for thou mayest be no longer steward."*

[**To elaborate** – A rich man, a business owner, finds out that one of his managers is abusing his privileges and essentially stealing from him, so he called him out and fired him.]

> **Vs. 3** *"Then the steward said within himself, What shall I do? for my lord taketh away from me the stewardship: I cannot dig; to beg I am ashamed."*
> **Vs. 4** *"I am resolved what to do, that, when I am put out of the stewardship, they may receive me into their houses."* **Vs. 5** *"So he called every one of his lord's debtors unto him, and said unto the first, How much owest thou unto my lord?"* **Vs. 6** *"And he said, An hundred measures of oil. And he said unto him, Take thy bill, and sit down quickly, and write fifty."* **Vs. 7** *"Then said he to another, And how much owest thou? And he said, An hundred measures of wheat. And he said unto him, Take thy bill, and write fourscore."*

[**To elaborate** – The fired manager says what am I going to do, I can't do anything else, I'm not strong enough to work a laboring job, and I'm too dignified to beg others for anything. So, he comes up with a plan to have his former clients' just pay back a percentage of what they owe to his boss. This will help to get back some of the money, and simultaneously get those that owe the debts to perhaps to like him.]

> **Vs. 8** *"And the lord commended the unjust steward, because he had done wisely: for the children of this world are in their generation wiser than the children of light."*

Verse 8 is the twist to the story and the point I want to focus on as we walk through this revelation. Jesus says that the rich man/ business owner **commended** what the fired manager did. I'm not sure every Christian reading this right now actually caught what Jesus Himself is conveying to us. See, this isn't something that is preached often in the church, if at all; this is not doctrinally accepted, but it is God's word. Jesus is saying plainly that the owner/ creator of the business literally praised this "unjust" crooked man for his reckless and renegade actions.

Now, just like some of you, I can maybe see forgiving this fired manager and not pressing charges on him, *but why would he go as far as commending him??* I hear you! This goes back to **_"…What we must do."_** This relates to the "work to eat" principle. I am not saying that this man was right for what he did. In truth, Jesus Himself was certainly not advocating that this man was right in what he had done. Jesus was simply saying that the man was right in working the principle. I know for some that's a difficult pill to swallow, so I need to you to take a deep breath and hear me.

Jesus, through this text, **does not** say that the man was <u>rewarded</u>, because that would have indicated something completely different. That would have said that the man was right in what he did, regardless of the principle. Instead, Jesus says that he was <u>commended</u>. In verse 8, Jesus tells us in His own words that the man was commended because he had acted <u>wisely</u>. So yes, according to this text, it is possible to act wisely without you yourself being wise. Just because you did something smart doesn't make you a smart person. As the idiom goes, "even a stopped clock is right twice a day." This is the distinct difference between <u>doing</u> good, and <u>being</u> good. See, you can *do* good and not *be* good, but it is impossible for you to *be* good and not *do* good. Selah!

As it relates to the revelation from this story, God says to His people that you should be like this man in his skillfulness and creativity to take care of himself. Just as Paul took care of himself when he was with those at the church of Thessalonica. Yet in this man's actions, we should also realize that we should not harm others in the process of being "skillful" and "creative;" this is one very important distinction for us to understand.

Matthew 10:16 *"Behold, I send you forth as sheep in the midst of wolves:* ___**be ye therefore wise as serpents, and harmless as doves**___*."* (KJV)

The fact that the man was <u>commended</u> and not <u>rewarded</u> helps to indicate that he didn't escape correction and/or punishment; rather, he was simply celebrated because he worked the principle. The principle is something that even some in the church don't bother to make an effort to operate within. God is seeking for us to somehow use this creativity and passion to work that which is good. He wants us to do good, to help others, and to be a witness for Him in everything that we do. Yet more often than not, there are Christians who may use the creative use of our skills, talents, and gifts to uncover all that is available for personal gain. Sound familiar? This is exactly what the fired manager did who was then commended, but not rewarded by God. In order to be rewarded, we need to use our skills, talents, and gifts to help others to achieve success as well. This is the work.

There is a particular passage of scripture where God points out that there are not enough workers in the church, those who call themselves Christians:

Matthew 9:37-38 Vs. 37 *"Then saith he unto his disciples, **The harvest truly is plenteous, but the labourers are few**;"* **Vs. 38** *"Pray ye therefore the Lord of the harvest, that he will send forth labourers into his harvest."* (KJV)

God is saying in this passage that there are plenty to be saved, plenty needing help, plenty crying out, but there are more pew/pulpit warmers and talkers in the church than there are actual workers. God is looking for the doers…

James 1:22-25 Vs. 22 *"**But be ye doers of the word, and not hearers only, deceiving your own selves**."* **Vs. 23** *"For if any be a hearer of the word, and not a doer, he is like unto a man beholding his natural face in a glass:"* **Vs. 24** *"For he beholdeth himself, and goeth his way, and straightway forgetteth what manner of man he was."* (KJV)

[**To elaborate** – If you are a hearer *(pew/pulpit warmer)* only and not a doer *(worker),* then you are lying to yourself about being a Christian.]

And the hard truth is that you're not even worthy to be <u>commended</u>, let alone be <u>rewarded</u>. God looks at you as even less than the crooked manager that we read about just a moment ago. Again, you can't say that you believe God, or even the call/ purpose of God that's on your life, if you are not willing to do the work that is assigned to that call. For as we quoted in Chapter 1…

James 2:26 *"For as the body without the spirit is dead, so **faith without works is dead** also."* (KJV)

As with most of the bible this is very clear. You can't believe in God if you don't have any works to that end. If I say I believe God, then I have to have works, or then according to the scripture my faith is dead—it simply does not exist. Furthermore, the bible says that…

Hebrews 11:6 *"But without faith it is **impossible** to please him: for **he that cometh to God must believe that he is, and that he is a rewarder** of them that diligently seek him."* (KJV)

There are many who say that they have Godly faith, but the litmus test is whether or not you have Godly works. Let me make this a little more practical: you can't say that you have Godly faith if you are only a listener of God, if you are only receiving from God, or if you are only leeching off of God's people. If at your core your only expectation is for God or others to do something, then you **DO NOT** have Godly faith, because you are lacking Godly works. You must be willing to pray but you must also be willing to participate in what you are praying about. Don't get this confused, I am not beating anyone up. I'm only admonishing us to "be" better, and not just "do" better. Because remember, you can "do" and not "be", but you cannot "be" and not "do".

Let's keep focused and use another great biblical example of what the work looks like, to be precise ***"…What we must do."*** Moses had a conversation with God (which in essence is prayer); during this particular conversation, Moses and the children of Israel were in a tough situation pitted between Pharaoh's army and the Red Sea.

> **Exodus 14:15-16 Vs. 15** *"And the Lord said unto Moses, Wherefore criest thou unto me?* **speak** *unto the children of Israel, that they* **go forward***"* **Vs. 16** *"But lift thou* **up thy rod, and stretch out thine hand over the sea**, *and divide it: and the children of Israel shall go on dry ground through the midst of the sea."* (KJV)

> **Exodus 14:21-22 Vs. 21** *"And **Moses stretched out his hand over the sea**; and the Lord caused the sea to go back by a strong east wind all that night, and made the sea dry land, and the waters were divided."* **Vs. 22** *"**And the children of Israel went into the midst of the sea upon the dry ground**: and the waters were a wall unto them on their right hand, and on their left."* (KJV)

These two passage of scripture speak to faith and works. Remember…

> **Romans 10:7** *"So then faith comes by hearing, and hearing by the word of God."*

Moses in Exodus 14:15-16 is hearing from God, thus his faith is being shaped and increased according to the scripture we just quoted. Shortly thereafter in Exodus 14:21-22, Moses is found participating and/or working what God had just recently instructed him to do. Now, here's the kicker. When you hear from God and work what He has said to you, then you shall have what He said. Let me simplify this as to be very clear: …you will have what He **said,**" not always what you want! In fact, God doesn't always tell you in detail what you will receive for doing what He said; nevertheless, we have to be mature enough to understand that whatever it is, it is good, because He is good.

I hope that this information is helping someone right now! Too many of us in the church today are just <u>listening</u> to preachers, and to others in the church telling us what God has said for us to do, and what God has said that we will receive from doing so. And yet, you as a believer have not heard from God concerning yourself?? I'm not saying that this is false teaching, or that the men or women of God can't hear from God concerning others. What I am saying is that if you are a believer in Christ, then your spirit should know if this is a message for you from God.

> **John 10:27-28 Vs. 27** *"<u>My sheep hear my voice, and I know them, and they follow me</u>:"* **Vs. 28** *"<u>And I give unto them eternal life; and they shall never perish, neither shall any man pluck them out of my hand.</u>"* (KJV)

If that is you, and you are just a hearer/ listener only, then I say to you, stop being blindly led through life by others. Just believe in God, believe in His word, do what you heard Him say, and you will receive what He said. Understand that you are not waiting on some sort of sign from God; YOU ARE the sign! ***You are a living sign***

We spend too much time "pretending" to be waiting on God, yet God is simply waiting on you to just do what He said to you in the first place. Stop waiting on a preacher to confirm what God said to you to do. Let what God said to you be the spark to get you to MOVE, and to work what He said. We should recognize that the word of God is immediate, it is quick, it is right now. Don't let someone preach to you stuff like "In the next 7 days, God is going to…", or "by this time tomorrow, God will show up." Think about this for a moment. If your spirit is struggling today, RIGHT NOW, then why in the world would you want a God that you have to wait 7 days for, or 3 days, or until sometime tomorrow, when God Himself has said that tomorrow is not promised (James 4:13-14)?? And God also has said…

> **Psalm 46:1** *"God is our refuge and strength, **a very present help** in trouble."* (KJV)

Let me give you a better visual to help digest that last nugget. My wife and I recently took our granddaughter to Sea World, and to their Aquatica Water Park. Long story short, we spent most of our time in the Roa's Rapids, a lazy river-type ride that uses water current to push and carry people in one direction throughout the "river" experience. We all had so much fun in the rapids, especially my granddaughter, I believe mainly because it was somewhat effortless and she just floated along. You may be asking how this is relevant to the nugget/ point I was just making on "right now vs. the next 7 days/ tomorrow." Well, let's break down the revelation that God gave me on this. There were two key areas that I was reminded of that were shown to me: 1) the rapids undercurrent is used to ensure that everyone in the rapids is flowing in one direction *(a unified flow)*. 2) God said the rapids already existed and had been working long before my family and I arrived at the park.

Here's the revelation… God's flow is unified, it is NOT new, and it is NOT in the future. His flow exists RIGHT NOW, and it existed before you showed up. In fact, we only show up because His flow exists, NOT to conjure it up when we need it. To reiterate something I said before, we are NOT waiting on God, God is waiting on us. The rapids of God's divine flow have to be stepped into, they have to be accessed. Remember Chapter One, *"Stop sitting on the dock of the bay …wasting time."*

See, making statements like "in the next 7 days…", etc., are often crutch statements that help to make preaching easier for certain preachers. They use these statements to have you kicking the can down the road, dangling the carrot just to keep you coming back. And thus, they subsequently don't have to be responsible to explain why what they said did not happen from one week to the next. <u>Now, in fairness to the preachers,</u> believers need to understand that the physical manifestation may not come about at the moment you hear God, or even right after you have done the work. Yet there should be an immediate shift, or change (a move) in your mind about the circumstance that gets you to work while awaiting the physical manifestation. See, you need to have done the work in order to do the work! Yes, the work has to be performed internally (inside of you) before it is physically manifested externally. I believe you are too smart not to know this for yourself already, so I don't feel I'm teaching this point. I'm only reaffirming it to you.

How can this be better explained? See, God is a spirit and before anything else was, He was. Therefore, spirit was first, then from the spirit came the natural. So it is with us. You have to believe inwardly first and then see yourself at the destination already, before you even book the ticket or call the Uber. Why would I, or anyone for that matter, book a ticket or call an Uber if I don't think that I was going to go anywhere? In my spirit, it is already so; I'm not waiting another week, another day, or another moment to convince myself that I am delivered. **At the time I hear God, I have faith in what He is saying**, and if I have "true" faith, then I must begin the works at the same time. And if I have works (using the example of booking a ticket) then I'm already convinced that I can go where He has said I can go, and I have what He said I can have. I don't need to see it physically right now to be convinced that it is already established spiritually; therefore, I know I will arrive at the destination that is printed on my ticket if I do the work of getting on the plane. Hello somebody!

2 Corinthians 5:7 *"(__For we walk by faith, not by sight:__)"* (KJV)

When we walk by faith, not by sight, what we are saying is that we don't care what it physically looks like right now. We believe in what we can see in our spirit and, therefore, we begin to govern our outward works accordingly. See, those in Christ walk by faith in Christ, not by what we can physically see. Therefore, we "do"/ work as if we already have the victory/ accomplishments. Thus, you will see true believers able to celebrate long before we have a physical manifestation in our lives of the victory. This is contrary to those who walk by sight and not by faith. All of this brings me to this point… **Whatever God says to do, we do it, as if we already know the outcome is victory.**

John 2:1-10 Vs. 1 *"And the third day there was a marriage in Cana of Galilee; and the mother of Jesus was there:"* Vs. 2 *"And both Jesus was called, and his disciples, to the marriage."* **Vs. 3** *"**And when they wanted wine**, the mother of Jesus saith unto him, **They have no wine**."* **Vs. 4** *"Jesus saith unto her, Woman, what have I to do with thee? mine hour is not yet come."* **Vs. 5** *"**His mother saith unto the servants, Whatsoever he saith unto you, do it**."* **Vs. 6** *"And there were set there six waterpots of stone, after the manner of the purifying of the Jews, containing two or three firkins apiece."* **Vs. 7** *"**Jesus saith unto them, Fill the waterpots with water. And they filled them up to the brim**."* **Vs. 8** *"**And he saith unto them, Draw out now, and bear unto the governor of the feast. And they bare it**."* **Vs. 9** *"When **the ruler of the feast had tasted the water that was made wine**, and knew not whence it was: (but the servants which drew the water knew;) the governor of the feast called the bridegroom,"* **Vs. 10** *"And saith unto him, Every* *man at the beginning doth set forth good wine; and*

when men have well drunk, then that which is

worse: but thou hast kept the good wine until now."

(KJV)

<Commercial Break…>

Now, before I get to the obvious point in this text of us doing what God says to do, let me say this one thing. To every churchgoer, to every preacher, to every Christian, I compel you to STOP trying to sugarcoat that Jesus turned water into WINE! This was not grape juice, as if Jesus doesn't know the difference?? *(He knows the difference, read Numbers 6:1-4)* It was wine (period/ full stop).

Now for this book, "Don't Pack, Just *Move*," I'm not getting dragged into the old debate of whether or not wine is okay to drink; this it is not the point that God has me driving home. I may take that up in the next book, but for now let's just stop misleading people with overly complex and inaccurate commentary. That said, I return to the theme of this book, which is in essence to have faith to move from one station in life to another. And yes, we should do so soberly.

<…and we're back>

The text in John 2 shows us yet again, as it did in the Exodus with Moses, and as it does in countless passages within the bible, that there is a relationship with God that requires participation, which for us is *"…What we must do."* The servants of God had, howbeit brief, a conversation with God, (again this is what defines prayer). The old saints use to sing "You will find a little talk with Jesus makes it right." And I would like to say that "a little talk with Jesus makes it work." The servants in this text had their conversation with Jesus, and then they immediately did what was said of them to do. They didn't wait "for 7 days", or "by this time tomorrow." No, they trusted Him (**now**), and they used their faith (**now**) so they could see something that they had never seen before (**now**). And thus, they were rewarded…

> **Hebrews 11:6** *"But without faith it is impossible to please him: for he that cometh to God must believe that he is, and that he is a **rewarder** of them that diligently seek him."* (KJV)

And as a result of the servants' faith in Jesus, they did witness a sign and wonder from Jesus as He turned water to wine right in front of them. And according to verse 10, it was the best wine, not some watered down version of wine. Additionally, it's important to note that Jesus could have done this without the servants, but instead He thought it best to have them <u>participate</u> in what they were about to see accomplished in their presence.

Now, being that this was the first recorded miracle of the earthly ministry of Jesus, everything about it sets precedent and thus becomes principle. Having said that, you must hear from God, you must perform the work God has assigned you, and then you will see what you have never seen before. Therefore, the last thing I want to address in this chapter, but certainly not the least, is…

"What God did…"

This portion of the chapter is even more exciting, and certainly more important than *"…What we must do,"* because we can't do what needs to be done without understanding first what He (God) has already done, finished and accomplished. This is imperative!

I'd like to dive into this section by just saying that everyone, believers and non-believers alike, everyone has a belief system, which is called their faith. I know most of us associate faith with religion and/or spirituality, but not so—faith is impartial. For instance, everyone believes that life comes from somewhere, and yet no one has physically seen the beginning of life. This is faith. Faith in its simplicity is a belief in an unseen thing, person, or God/ a god. Now whether we exercise our faith for God or for ourselves, we need to understand that the power of our faith and the power to exercise our faith both come from God.

There is uncommon use of faith, which is Godly faith, and there is common use of faith, which is superficial and self-rewarding. "Common use" is what is given to everybody at physical birth. Therefore, it is a choice of everyone to stay common, or to grow into the "uncommon." See, common use faith is used in our everyday life, such as some of the instances in chapter one where we mentioned that *"no one attempts to sit in a seat unless they first believe that the chair is there. And no one tries to turn on a TV unless they first have a belief that the TV will display a picture."*

Common use faith can also be used to execute certain biblical principles; doing so **will** yield to you what God has declared it would *("sowing & reaping," "work & eat," etc.)*. To make this even more clear, if you get a job, go to work, pay your bills (on time), stay out of overwhelming debt, and establish savings, then you, too, can have good credit. You, too, can buy a house; you, too, can buy a nice car; you, too, can take exotic vacations; and yes, you, too, can start a business. None of this requires faith in Jesus. If it did, then Muslims wouldn't have these things. Buddhists wouldn't have these things. Heck, for that matter atheists wouldn't have these things either. Would you agree?

See, these things only require what I call "common use" faith—if you believe that you have the ability to succeed and you apply yourself, then you will likely see success (whatever that means to you). See common use faith is shallow because its only purpose is to selfishly seek 'things' as its chief objective. With common use faith, seeking "things" for personal benefit is the product, and helping others may be a by-product. However, with "uncommon use" faith, seeking God (helping others, and growing in God's wisdom) is the product and the "things" are by-products.

> **Matthew 6:33** *"But seek ye first the kingdom of God, and his righteousness; and all these things shall be added unto you."* (KJV)

God doesn't get caught up on fashion, big houses, luxury vehicles, or the like. Nevertheless, He allowed those things to be created, and thus He makes them available to us all. Yet, just because it is not wrong to have these things doesn't immediately make it good for us to have them.

> **1 Corinthians 10:23** *"All things are lawful for me, but all things are not expedient: all things are lawful for me, but all things edify not."* (KJV)

See, the things that are good for us are the things that are in God's will for our lives. Again, these are the things that are good for us. So, is money good for us? Of course; the real question is how much money is good for each of us to have? Some can hit the lottery and they can do some great things with it to glorify God, help others, and invest for future generations. And then others can hit the lottery and within a year die from a drug overdose, or use the money to oppress others.

I'm going into great detail on the earthly benefits of doing things God's way vs. our way, because most in the church often confuse what is achieved through Godly faith with what can be achieved by anyone through common faith. Some in the church often have three flawed beliefs: **1)** We don't think that a measure of faith is given to everyone irrespective of spiritual belief; this is what we're taught. **2)** We believe that our faith is to obtain "things," as if that is the core purpose. **3)** If we have faith, then we believe that this is synonymous with blessings.

See, those with uncommon use faith realize that the "things" we get are temporary and not eternal. Money comes and goes, cars rust out, houses fall apart, and jets get decommissioned, so these cannot be primary. Therefore, the focus has to be on things that are eternal and not of this world, or we truly die when those things die. Equally, we should focus on the work more so then the reward. And seeing, therefore, that the reward is just the byproduct of the work, it then becomes uninspiring and unimaginable that the reward should also be the motive. Make the focus on doing the work of God and not the reward of God, knowing that the reward is a given based on the work. God declared the following…

Ephesians 1:3 *<u>"Blessed be the God and Father of our Lord Jesus Christ, who hath blessed us with all spiritual blessings in heavenly places in Christ:"</u>* (KJV)

<u>What</u> <u>God</u> <u>did</u> <u>was</u> <u>give</u> <u>us</u> <u>His</u> <u>Son</u> <u>Jesus</u> <u>Christ</u>. I can stop there, because truly those 10 words could have been the whole chapter. In fact, those words could have been the whole book. What God did was give us every spiritual blessing (or reward) in high places through His Son Christ Jesus. This means that God does not directly concern Himself with, nor puts emphasis on, giving us the natural/ temporal things; rather, He seeks to empower us with the things of the spirit, those things that are eternal, and harness the power by which all these natural things are able to come into being.

When we say that we have faith in God, what we are declaring is that we have faith in what God Himself has done. And that, in essence, is the grounds by which we can declare who God is. So when I say through this chapter, *"What God did…,"* I am effectively saying

EVERYTHING!!! And through His accomplished word/work, He has

empowered us to not only understand *"What we must do…,"* but through

His Son Christ Jesus He has given us the power to do it completely.

CHAPTER FIVE

"What are you talking about?"

This chapter begins by storming out of the gate and asking us all a profound question, "What are you talking about?" This is not only a good question, but seeing that most of what we do in life can be categorized as some form of communication, it should also be something that forces us to self-examine ourselves. Self-examine how, and what we find ourselves talking about. Is it positive? Is it constructive? Will it bring us any closer to our holistic success, or our destiny? These are some of the hard but key questions that we must ask ourselves in order to make progress in our desire to move in this life; helping us become conscious of what we are communicating and to whom we are communicating with, will be critical as we seek holistic success in this life. And just to reiterate what was said in our earlier chapters, we are defining "success" simply as *one being in a position to help others*. This gives us the understanding that if we can help others, then we would have already arrived at a position to have more than what we need. This would be as much spiritual as it is emotional, physical, and even financial. After all, how can you help someone pay their light bill if you don't have enough to pay yours?

Taking all of this into account, this chapter is meant to be straightforward, without restrictions or parameters. In other words, if any of this hurts you while you are reading it, then just say OUCH!! But whatever you do, <u>don't stop reading</u>!

NOW LET'S GO ALL IN ON THIS CHAPTER...

The scripture focus for this chapter will be the New Testament text which is often referred to as "The Road to Emmaus." It describes an encounter of two men who are found interacting with Jesus shortly after His resurrection.

Luke 24:13-35 Vs. 13 *And, behold, two of them went that same day to a village called Emmaus, which was from Jerusalem about threescore furlongs.* **Vs. 14** *And they talked together of all these things which had happened.* **Vs. 15** *And it came to pass, that, while they communed together and reasoned, Jesus himself drew near, and went with them.* **Vs. 16** *But their eyes were holden that they should not know him.* **Vs. 17** *And he said unto them, What manner of communications are these that ye have one to another, as ye walk, and are sad?* **Vs. 18** *And the one of them, whose name was Cleopas, answering said unto him, Art thou only a stranger in Jerusalem, and hast not known the things which are come to pass there in these days?*

> **Vs. 19** *And he said unto them, What things? And they said unto him, Concerning Jesus of Nazareth, which was a prophet mighty in deed and word before God and all the people*: **Vs. 20** *And how the chief priests and our rulers delivered him to be condemned to death, and have crucified him.* **Vs. 21** *But we trusted that it had been he which should have redeemed Israel: and beside all this, to day is the third day since these things were done.* **Vs. 22** *Yea, and certain women also of our company made us astonished, which were early at the sepulchre;* **Vs. 23** *And when they found not his body, they came, saying, that they had also seen a vision of angels, which said that he was alive.* **Vs. 24** *And certain of them which were with us went to the sepulchre, and found it even so as the women had said: but him they saw not.* (KJV)

This is a great story that gives all of us an understanding of how immensely important it is that we don't get distracted by the "things" and circumstances that surround us. It keeps us from focusing our attention on what/who really matters, and keeps us from seeing our victory for what/who it really is. This story and these two men are great examples, as they were on their way to a place called Emmaus and they were conversing with each other about the things that had just recently happened in Jerusalem. And while on their way to Emmaus, their response to what had happen in Jerusalem was negative, a response of disappointment, and one of hopelessness. They were so dismayed to the point that they couldn't recognize the great victory that had just taken place, even though the victory was so close that it was literally walking right next to them. In fact, their victory was so close that it was actually talking to them.

Vs. 25 *Then he said unto them, O fools, and slow of heart to believe all that the prophets have spoken*: **Vs. 26** *Ought not Christ to have suffered these things, and to enter into his glory?* **Vs. 27** *And beginning at Moses and all the prophets, he expounded unto them in all the scriptures the things concerning himself.* **Vs. 28** *And they drew nigh unto the village, whither they went: and he made as though he would have gone further.* **Vs. 29** *But they constrained him, saying, Abide with us: for it is* *toward evening, and the day is far spent. And he went in to tarry with them.* **Vs. 30** *And it came to pass, as he sat at meat with them, he took bread, and blessed it, and brake, and gave to them.* **Vs. 31** *And their eyes were opened, and they knew him; and he vanished out of their sight.* **Vs. 32** *And they said one to another, Did not our heart burn within us, while he talked with us by the way, and while he opened to us the scriptures*? (KJV)

One thing all of us should recognize is that if you talk to God long enough, you will realize your faults and then begin to change your thinking and your dialogue. These two men started out their journey with a conversation that was negative, disappointing, and hopeless. However, by the end of their journey they felt fired up and encouraged as they heard Jesus speak, reminding them that victory didn't leave them, that they left the victory. Not so much the place per se, even though the place was Jerusalem and it did represent where Jesus' earthly ministry concluded and He established His finished work. Nevertheless, Jerusalem is still only metaphorically being spoken of for this revelation, because Jesus never truly left the two men, since we understand Him to be Omnipresent (everywhere at the same time). Thus, Jesus didn't leave the two men; rather, the two men left Jesus *(Jerusalem)* and then became sad.

Herein is a glorious revelation of the spirit, and that is this: Jesus will not leave us nor forsake us. As a result, He is always there for a convenient conversation to help us find our way back to him. This is similar to our focus scripture text that opened chapter two speaking of the young man who came to himself in the pig pen and then returned home to his father.

Reminder…

> **Vs. 33** *And they rose up the same hour, and returned to Jerusalem, and found the eleven gathered together, and them that were with them,* **Vs. 34** *Saying, The Lord is risen indeed, and hath appeared to Simon.* **Vs. 35** *And they told what things were done in the way, and how he was known of them in breaking of bread.* (KJV)

This text in Luke 24 boils down to Jesus saying (paraphrasing), "what are you talking about? What has caused you to lose hope? And why do you feel like you've been let down?" And when we find ourselves being negative, talking in disappointment, having conversation without hope, Jesus is saying the same thing to us all: don't you know what I have done for you, what my death, burial, and resurrection has given unto you? If so, then why are you so discouraged, why are you so stressed and wandering around as if lost, having meaningless conversations? Jesus is saying *(continuing with my paraphrasing)* "I promised this would happen, because you needed it to happen. I died that you might have life, and that you may have life more abundantly."

For some of you reading this right now, I'm sure that this may all sound crazy, and you may not even believe in who Jesus is, or what He has done for you. However, even with your belief, you still have to agree that at minimum, your communication not only exposes your heart, but it is also significantly important to your progress. Therefore, this brings us to the key point of revelation in this chapter, which is that our communication has to be focused and deliberate at all times, seeing that it is significant to our progress. So, appreciating that our communication is so multifaceted, we can talk with our voice, with our hands, with our body language, with our fashion, and yes we can even talk with our silence. In addition to these obvious methods of communication, we also speak through our works. These are several valid forms of communication, and yet some don't even know what they are saying when they are "conversing." Selah!

For example, with fashion we see young men walking around with their pants half pulled down off their waist, not even knowing what the original purpose of this statement comes from. They don't even know that those who started this "trend" started it while they were locked away in prison. The point of this "trend" was to communicate to other men that they were available for sex without verbally stating it out loud, for fear of negative consequences. This origin story in and of itself should change the minds of some who wear this "style" to consider a change, and/or a move in their thinking. Yet, before we judge these young men and their lack of fashion sense, or judge these two men on the road to Emmaus, let's take a quick peek at some of the communication that we may be having.

What are some of the things that we say, or have said, that may make as much sense as what others have intentionally, or unintentionally communicated? Some of us may have complained about our spouses, our jobs, neighbors, churches, and some may have even complained about God Himself. Now with the exception of complaining about God, let me give you my definition of complaining, versus compliant. Both are alike in the sense that both can boldly declare the facts of the reality being faced by an individual. However, based on my experience, when someone complains, they are usually describing a problem that they are too lazy to solve themselves, and therefore they are hoping that those who hear it will solve for it instead. In other words, they are just going to sit in this "pig pen" and complain about their situation, but they are not going to consult God, or work any of His principles to **MOVE** out of the mess themselves.

Conversely, when someone is what I'm calling "compliant," they will not only boldly declare the facts, but they are <u>obedient</u> to consult with God and work His principles to bring about resolution. Complaining without a solution is just another weight we are packing in our bags that hold us back from holistic "success." It also communicates a hopeless and negative message to others who are stuck in their own pig pens, or mess. I see this as a distinct and utterly important difference, because one says I'm just going to believe (have faith) that this will be fixed somehow; the other says I'm going to believe (have faith) that this will be fixed, and then takes the opportunity to apply the wisdom to overcome the challenge (works). That all being said, **<u>there is nothing wrong</u>** with boldly declaring what the reality of a situation is, even if the situation looks very bleak, as long as you have a viable solution that you are working. In this case, you are only stating the facts of that moment/ season you are in. But those of us who know God, and know who He has made us to be, cannot be found simply "complaining."

The goal, then, is for us to always be found, in every form of our communication, talking <u>with the understanding</u> of what took place in

Jerusalem. That is to say, talking <u>with the understanding</u> of what Christ has done for us all, empowering us with the ability to impact, influence, and change the world!

Now let's take some time and directly address some of the things that we may hear, or have even said in the church. Some of the things that are mentioned by those in the church that may have either been said, prayed, preached, or sung, and yet may not have been completely accurate or even helpful to those seeking change. Things that might make even Jesus say, "What are you talking about?"

Here are a few of the most common things said:

Eyes have not seen, nor have ears heard what God has prepared for you.

I thought I would start with this one, because I believe this is one of the most popular phrases used by churchgoers today. This is one of the phrases that can be classified as a "half-truth," which actually means that it's not true at all. This saying/ cliché is spoken by many all around the world. And the scripture that is often used to attempt to justify this cliché is:

1 Corinthians 2:9 "***But as it is written, Eye hath not seen, nor ear heard***, *neither have entered into*

> *the heart of man, **the things which God hath***
>
> ***prepared for them that love him**.*" (KJV)

This scripture, when taken out of context, is misused to underpin the misleading perception that we have no revelation of what God wants for our lives. Churchgoers habitually say this to one another when they are trying to comfort, and/or encourage someone who is holding out hope for something or someone. It is also fraudulently used to "prophesy" to someone when the person prophesying has no idea what to say or predict. It alludes that God has something for you, something great, and something that can only be shared with you, **BUT** God chooses not to show you, only to watch you agonize in your anxiety. Wait—What?? However, we know that this is not the God that most of us reading this book serve. So, if we were to read the full context of this verse, then we should have also included verse 10 which states,

> *"**But God hath revealed them unto us by his***
>
> ***Spirit**: for the Spirit searcheth all things, yea, the*
>
> *deep things of God."* (KJV)

Verse 10 is **HUGELY** important to this passage because when this is included, it changes the whole dynamic and understanding of this frequently misquoted text. When I read verses 9 and 10 together, they reveal to me that we are not as blind as those who only quote verse 9 would like us all to believe. In fact, to the contrary—when we read these verses together, we learn that God reveals to us *(those that love Him)* what He has prepared for us, what He has purposed for us to enjoy. So the next time you hear someone say ***"But as it is written, Eye hath not seen, nor ear heard***, *neither have entered into the heart of man,* ***the things which God hath prepared for them that love him,***" but don't finish with ***"But God hath revealed them unto us by his Spirit***: *for the Spirit searcheth all things, yea, the deep things of God,"* just ask them "what are you talking about?" And then proceed to enlighten them with the whole truth in the text which includes verse 10, but do this in a loving, and sincere manner. Don't go acting like you know everything, because chances are as we go through some of these other sayings/ clichés, you may find that you yourself need to be further enlightened. ☺

Praying that God will move our mountains.

Most Christians see God more as a vessel to fulfill good works, and not as the source from whence the power to perform the works comes from. We forget, or are sometimes uneducated in the church concerning our faith, thus we sit around *(on the docks of our bay)* waiting on God to "move our mountains." Yet God didn't intend to do all the work. In fact,

142

His word makes it quite clear, on several accounts, that we have work to do ("good" works).

Ephesians 2:8-10 Vs. 8 *"For by grace are ye saved through faith; and that not of yourselves: it is the gift of God:"* **Vs. 9** *"Not of works, lest any man should boast."* **Vs. 10** ***"For we are his workmanship, created in Christ Jesus unto good works****, which God hath before ordained that we should walk in them."* (KJV)

Matthew 5:16 *"Let your light so shine before men, that they may see **your good works**, and glorify your Father which is in heaven."* (KJV)

Galatians 6:9 ***"And let us not be weary in well doing****: for in due season we shall reap, if we faint not."* (KJV)

Colossians 3:23-24 Vs. 23 ***"And whatsoever ye do, do it heartily, as to the Lord, and not unto men****;"* **Vs. 24** *"Knowing that of the Lord ye shall receive the reward of the inheritance: for ye serve the Lord Christ."* (KJV)

143

Therefore, seeing that we can (and that we often do) speak with both our works AND our non-works, what is it then that we find ourselves communicating? Are we saying that we can be used to accomplish works (to move mountains), or are we communicating that we are the source that gives power to accomplish the works? If we are communicating through our "non-works," then we are essentially proclaiming that we are the source, because by default the source gives the power to those who perform the works. So then, are we saying that we are responsible for giving the power, or are we saying we are responsible for using/ applying the power?

If you are still wondering about your position and role in the Kingdom, then let's look at one more scripture which will help us clear this up.

> **Matthew 17:20** *"And Jesus said unto them,*
>
> *Because of your unbelief: for verily I say unto you,*
>
> ***If ye have faith as a grain of mustard seed, ye shall***
>
> ***say unto this mountain, Remove hence to yonder***
>
> ***place; and it shall remove; and nothing shall be***
>
> ***impossible unto you.***" (KJV)

So, what we can plainly see through this scripture is that God is our source, because it is He who has given to us His word, *"Jesus said unto them…,"* and then if they/ you/ I do what He says, then by default we are doing the work. The scripture says that *"you shall say unto this mountain…"* Remember, *"But be ye doers of the word, and not hearers only…"*

In summary, let's stop waiting on God to speak to our mountains for us, when in fact He has empowered us to speak to and move these ourselves. Remember in Chapter One when we were discussing the man at the pool of Bethesda, that one of the first points I made was **Moving is the key!** Moving is an action and thus it is a work, and if God said to do it, then it is a Godly work.

Just let go, and let God!

This one is not a friend, or akin to "faith without works." This cliché is typically spoken to us by others when we are going through a storm (metaphorically speaking). It suggests that we should stop trying to overcome the challenges and just kick back and rely on God to do it for us. This is similar to the first saying that we looked at about moving mountains. We often believe that God will do something for us without understanding that He will often do it through us.

When we read a text like…

Revelation 12:11 *"And they overcame him by the blood of the Lamb, and by the word of their testimony; and they loved not their lives unto the death."* (KJV)

…many focus on the first half of the text and say that this justifies that we should just let go and let God, because it's only about the blood of Jesus and by our words. And though the blood of Jesus is, in fact, an absolute truth in this text, it is our understanding of the "our words" part that we don't completely have accurate. See read the text again in its entirety reading the first part and the second part closely. Again yes, whether in this text, or in fact any text in the bible, Jesus is the preeminent point (period/ full stop). It is by Jesus that we have the ability to do anything in this life, as the bible states…

Acts 17:28 *"**For in him we live, and move, and have our being**; as certain also of your own poets have said, For we are also his offspring."* (KJV)

The next part of Revelations 12:11 states, "… *and by the word of their testimony;*" This speaks very openly to our communication to the world of who God is and what He has done for us, both for us to be here in the earth, and to be alive. Coupling that with *"…and they loved not their lives unto the death*," we can see that the text does not speak to "our word" per se, but more to our testimony, our holistic communication of who God is. And we do this through our voice, our hands, our body language, our fashion, or as we said earlier, by our works and even our silence. This is the word of our testimony, or the word we bare record of, it doesn't mean that we do nothing, or that we just **"let go."** It actually means just the opposite. It means that we should not love things, or even our own lives more than we love to speak about and holistically communicate our appreciation and witness love for God. After all, it is God who has given us the power to be His witnesses and to have success. Having that in mind, we are obligated to "let go" and move forward in life because of what God has done; therefore I don't say ~~"Let go, and let God!"~~ I say, ***"Let go for God!"***

Name it, and Claim it / Blab it, and Grab it!

I believe that these two clichés mislead Christians more than any other. This is mainly because the premise behind these sayings is that all you have to do is say it and it will happen for you. This is likely the laziest form of religious "action" that exists across any religion. There are so many people within the church today who choose to use these two clichés because, quite frankly, it's easy. It's an easy way to blame God for when we don't get what we are naming, or blabbing to receive. It's an easy way to kick the can down the road and not accept the responsibility of participating in what you are seeking to receive. This method does not suggest that we even seek God for what we are declaring; we just name what we want and it appears (poof!). So, if we name someone else's spouse, or someone else's house, or maybe someone else's job, then it/they will be ours??

I hope you can see how twisted and how clearly absurd this philosophy is to operate under. This means that we can have what we wish to be granted to us all simply because we want what we want! Unfortunately, churchgoers are often the ones lulled, or pacified, into a deep sleep (chapter two) that keeps them from a conscious reality. Now, in fairness to this topic, speaking what God has said is not out of line; in fact, it is very much in line and is called prophesy. This actually has several origins in scripture for believers to understand and accept. However, like anything else in scripture, it is always necessary to be placed into context. This is actually something we will be looking at in the next chapter. As for this cliché, since it is based on nothing but a person's superficial wants and cravings and has no basis in God's truth, I say to you, please stop naming and claiming, blabbing and grabbing!

CHAPTER SIX

"STOP Talking so Much!"

149

As we wind down our time together in "Don't Pack, Just *Move!*" let's look at something else that we can sometimes carry around as baggage that hinders our progress in life. Now you will find that the contents in this chapter are akin to the chapter we just read. The last chapter delivered great points about communication and how we often say things that have no merit in supporting our journey forward. And anything that doesn't take us closer to our purpose and destiny has a propensity to take us further away.

In this chapter, we will continue to look at communication, but in a more in-depth manner. I seek to show how verbal and actionable communication (our work) go hand and hand; how what we speak has to be backed up with action. This, by comparison, will be a shorter chapter, but that should not diminish the revelation it provides. Having that in mind, let's just jump into our focused text to help best illustrate this part of the revelation.

Ezekiel 37:1-14 Vs. 1 *"The hand of the Lord was upon me, and carried me out in the spirit of the Lord, and **set me down in the midst of the valley which was full of bones**,"* **Vs. 2** *"And caused me to pass by them round about: and, behold, there were very many in the open valley; and, lo, they were* *very dry.*" **Vs. 3** "*And **he said unto me, Son of man, can these bones live?** And I answered, O Lord God, thou knowest.*" **Vs. 4** "*Again **he said unto me, Prophesy upon these bones,** and say unto them, O ye dry bones, hear the word of the Lord.*" **Vs. 5** "*Thus saith the Lord God unto these bones; Behold, I will cause breath to enter into you, and ye shall live:*" **Vs. 6** "*And I will lay sinews upon you, and will bring up flesh upon you, and cover you with skin, and put breath in you, and ye shall live; and ye shall know that I am the Lord.*"   (Continued below)

[**To elaborate** – This text is a harmonious look at the revelation God gave to His prophet Ezekiel and the obedience which Ezekiel gave to God. This is the essence of the type of relationship that is desired and required by God for every believer. And so, as we begin this text, we find God showing Ezekiel a valley which was full of bones, and the bones were said to be very dry. This detail is important, because if the bones are very dry, it would indicate that even the marrow within the bone has decomposed. And if the marrow has dried, then the bones would be an indication that the person whose bones they were had died months or even years ago. This would indicate that the person

is so dead that the bones are well beyond being resuscitated back to life.

God then proceeds to ask Ezekiel a straightforward yet profound

question, can these bones live? Most of us would say that this is a simple

question, until we opened our mouth to answer, at which time we would

likely begin to wonder and question within ourselves whether or not our first

gut response was truly the right response. Ezekiel cleverly answers by just

saying *(paraphrasing)* "you know better than I do whether or not these bones

will live." God says to Ezekiel *(paraphrasing)* "I want you to speak my word

to these bones and tell them that they will live, and also tell them how I am

going to cause this to happen. And before you finish speaking my words to

these bones, also let them know that through these actions they will know that

I am the Lord."]

Here is what I want to say about this before going any further. I

titled this chapter "STOP Talking so Much!" because I wanted to be clear

on what God did and did not say to Ezekiel. I believe in doing so, this will

help us to better understand what God is instructing us to do, and what He

is **not** instructing us to do. God said to His prophet Ezekiel, "prophesy

upon these bones," but He did not say "talk" to these bones. This is

important. See, when someone "prophesies," they are to merely speak

what God has instructed them to say. And since this is <u>speaking,</u> not talking, it signifies that this is a more official task, and a more one-sided communication. This is why professional "speakers" are not called "talkers," and why their engagements are not called "talking engagements," but rather "speaking engagements." Therefore, speaking is notably recognized in professional circles as one-sided communication.

Conversely, when someone is talking, it implies that it's a more casual/ informal discussion, or a dialog which typically includes multiple people. This distinction helps us to both better grasp the title of this bonus chapter **"STOP Talking so Much!"** and, more importantly, it helps us to grow in our knowledge of how to apply God's word. **Next…**

> **Vs. 7** *"**So I prophesied as I was commanded: and as I prophesied, there was a noise, and behold a shaking, and the bones came together, bone to his bone.**"* **Vs. 8** *"And when I beheld, lo, the sinews and the flesh came up upon them, and the skin covered them above: but there was no breath in them."* **Vs. 9** *"**Then said he unto me, Prophesy unto the wind,** prophesy, son of man, and say to the wind, Thus saith the Lord God; Come from the four winds, **O breath, and breathe upon these slain, that they may live.**"* **Vs. 10** *"**So I prophesied as he**

> ***commanded me, and the breath came into them,
> and they lived, and stood up upon their feet, an
> exceeding great army.***"

[**To elaborate** – Ezekiel was someone who trusted God, had faith in God, and therefore he did what God commanded of him to do. And immediately, during his obedience, he began to see the bones themselves begin to work and come together, not just in a pile or in some random fashion, but the bones came together reuniting with the appropriate bone from the appropriate person. The marrow came back, the tissue and muscles was renewed, the organs were redeveloped, the skin was laid upon the tissue and muscles, yet the body was still dead.]

Let me make one point here. Many of us are like these bones/bodies. We allow the word of God to call us out and command us to participate in unifying the pieces of our lives back together, but we often do not sit long enough to become alive. Allow me to say it another way: many of us only sit under the word long enough to look good, but won't sit long enough to become alive. Selah!

I hope you are hearing this, because it is HUGELY IMPORTANT that we do not leave God just because we feel like we have arrived at a certain point in our existence. Some of us start going to church and learning the principles of God, and we get a good feeling as we jump and shout, but before we can grow, we turn away. You know who they are! They go to church service they begin to start feeling some peace and comfort, but before they can absorb it and properly apply the word to their life, they meet a significant other that would rather go to breakfast or brunch rather than go to church. Or perhaps your significant other declares date night each week on the days that you typically went to bible study. Or maybe you got that new car and now you prefer to watch the service on an online stream while washing the car instead of physically going to church service.

We have to let the word work in us long enough to the point where we begin to let it work out of us; thus, we will begin to unpack the weights of our past and begin to move into our future. This portion of text ends by declaring that when we hear the word and/or sit under the word long enough, we will become what the word declares. God reveals to Ezekiel that once He breathed into the empty bodies, they not only became alive again, but they stood up on their feet as an exceedingly great army. Understand that when Ezekiel was exposed to them, they were dead, scattered bones with no organs, muscles, tissue, or even bone marrow. In fact, they were likely killed in some type of battle based on the way the bones were scattered, and seeing that when God saved them/ birthed them, the text says that He did so making them an exceedingly great army.

155

Can I just state the obvious here? When we are born again in Christ, we are born as an exceedingly great army. This means that we were an army that was ultimately defeated, but when we were born again we were an exceedingly great army, which means that we were not to be defeated again. ***Next...***

Vs. 11 *"Then he said unto me, Son of man, these bones are the whole house of Israel: behold, they say, Our bones are dried, and our hope is lost: we are cut off for our parts."* **Vs. 12** ***"Therefore prophesy and say unto them****, Thus saith the Lord God; Behold, O my people,* **I will open your graves, and cause you to come up out of your graves, and bring you into the land of Israel.***"* **Vs. 13** *"And ye shall know that I am the Lord, when I have opened your graves, O my people, and brought you up out of your graves,"* **Vs. 14** *"And shall put my spirit in you, and ye shall live, and I shall place you in your own land: then shall ye know that I the Lord have spoken it, and performed it, saith the Lord."* (KJV)

156

[To elaborate – Now, something I want to make sure that we highlight and underscore in this passage of scripture, because it is acutely important. God instructed Ezekiel to prophesy to the bones, which God later declares in verse 11 to be the whole house of Israel. One of the most important things to remember is Ezekiel himself is a part of the house of Israel. Thus, what we should not miss is that Ezekiel was not only prophesying to his immediate family, relatives, and friends, but **he was ALSO prophesying to himself**. So, having that in mind, we should always remember to speak God's word over our own lives, our own valley of bones, even as we prophesy/speak what God is declaring to others.

Considering the above, what God is showing in this last part of the focus text is that everything He was allowing Ezekiel to see was designed to show him God's rebirth for His people. God reveals to Ezekiel, and ultimately to all of us, through this text, that you or areas in your life may be dead, or even look dead], but remember…

John 14:6 *"**Jesus saith unto him, I am** the way, the truth, **and the life**: no man cometh unto the Father, but by me."* (KJV)

What God requires us to do in order for lives to be changed, and for the world to be better, is for us to **"STOP Talking so Much!"** and start prophesying more. Stop <u>talking</u> to your lack, or dead situations, and start speaking what God has said for you to speak concerning these matters. And if you are not sure what it is God is saying to speak, then read His word, study His word, and trust His word. Holistic success is available to those who are willing to access it by faith *(faith without works is dead)*.

After all of this, this is what I can say to you…

- Don't pack what you used to believe was possible, don't pack the limitation that you and others have put on yourself.

- Don't pack what you've been taught about spirituality, but experience God for yourself.

- Don't pack your failures, but keep working the principles of God.

Listen, get off the dock of the bay, and understand what you have in order to get what you want. Allow yourself to have multiple streams of income, and don't settle for a church that doesn't teach the same. Appreciate what God has done in order for you to better appreciate what you are supposed to do. Don't let yourself get distracted with daily cares—your job, your boss, negative co-workers, financial difficulties, doctors' reports, etc. These are the things that can keep our eyes off Jesus and cause us to begin to talk more about the things than about the one who gives us power to change our circumstances. Remember we must have faith and works, and we must do more speaking of God's word and less talking about our ideas and what *we* think will be best.

CHAPTER SEVEN
BONUS

"FINAL NUGGETS"

Now, in this grand finale of "Don't Pack, Just *Move!*" we are going to look at a different angle, thus attempting to cover every relevant aspect on this topic. We have spent the bulk of our time speaking about getting our mind and spirit right, because without those things we can't consistently move forward physically/ naturally. However, I would like to focus a good portion of this last part on the excessive physical packing that some of us do, and how it holds us back from further "success" as it is defined in this book.

Let me start by say something that may seem off topic, but just go with me for a moment. The self-storage industry is, and has been, one of the fasted growing businesses in the market for years. This is an interesting fact and can only be attributed to the fact that more and more people are accumulating more than what they have the capacity to keep in the place where they live. These days more people are packing too much and therefore it makes moving from one place to another that much more difficult. And some need to recognize that there are things that cannot go where we want to live. For instance, some want to move from poverty stricken community into a wealthy gated community. However, in your current community you may have torn screens in your windows, worn out lawn furniture, and a car in your driveway sitting on cinder blocks. ***THIS WILL NOT BE ALLOWED*** in your new wealthier gated community. It may play good in movies, and TV shows, but trust me it does not work in real life.

That said, let me remind us that we must change our mental/ spiritual position, change our thoughts to God's thoughts so we can change our physical position to where God wants us to be. This is the place where we can make the most impact, because if we keep a poor and broke mindset, then we will never truly be wealthy. Sure, we may obtain money, and perhaps lots of it, but never fulfilling our purpose, never impacting the world as we were intended. Say it now: I CHANGED MY MIND… I am not poor, I am not broke, I am not insignificant, but I am wealthy, I am my brother's keeper, I am fulfilling God's purpose for my life to impact the lives of others in a positive and profound way. I am a member of the body of Christ and I need God and I need you, just as you need God and you need me. MY MIND HAS BEEN CHANGED!

> **Proverbs 23:7** *__For as he thinketh in his heart, so is he:__ Eat and drink, saith he to thee; but his heart is not with thee.* " (KJV)

Now, somewhat continuing on the theme of the self-storage facilities… I remember talking to God one day and saying that if I just had a little more money, I could <u>do this and do that</u>. And God said something to me that I will never forget. He plainly said, ***<u>"Maybe it's not that you don't have enough, maybe it's that you have too much</u>.***" This statement troubled me, and yet was extremely profound. It brought me to a moment of clarity, as it related to financial stewardship. See, the simple revelation here is that most of us believe a simple principle—that we could do more if we just had more. This is not an incorrect principle; in fact, it is very much accurate, but what's easily missed in this is the question, is it possible to do more with what we currently have? And the answer that God gave me, and the answer for most of us reading this, is an emphatic YES!

God said, ***<u>"Maybe it's not that you don't have enough, maybe it's that you have too much</u>.***" In other words, what He was saying to me was that I may not have more than I can afford, but I have more than I need. See, He wasn't asking a question. Rather, He was making a statement, saying that if I were to get rid of some of the things I don't need, then I would realize that I already have more than enough to "do this, and do that."

Let me make this more practical… Someone may be single and he/she may have a nice one-bedroom condo, a luxury vehicle, and taking perhaps two exotic trips a year and still have money to help others. And then, making the same money, he/she upgrades to a 3 bedroom single family house, and takes three exotic trips a year. Now you find yourself saying that you need more in order to continue to help others. However, is that really true, or is it that you now just have more going out then you do coming in? Most of us always have enough to help someone else, but we may not realize it because we have too much going out, or too much that we are holding on to. If we think about it, many of us are the reason why the self-storage industry is one of the fast growing businesses.

OR in another practical scenario… Perhaps you simply have too much, because sometimes when you have too much you can find yourself getting into things that you wouldn't otherwise have access to get into. You could find yourself getting into infidelity, into drugs, into activities that could cause you to be too busy to help others or too busy to spend time with God or family. ***"Maybe it's not that you don't have enough, maybe it's that you have too much".*** See how this works?

Sometimes you have to downsize in order to move up; sometimes you have to refrain from packing and/or keeping storage of the excessive items in order to move, and to move quickly. See, when opportunities come your way, and they will come your way because they come to everyone, you will not be able to move quickly enough to take advantage of them. So, don't pack things you don't need, **AND** get rid of people who you have accumulated that do not reciprocate your support, because you will undoubtedly miss your opportunities.

Allow me to be transparent for a moment and talk about me. I don't have a full blown energetic celebration when I outwardly see something good happen in my life, because I know that I've already spent time energetically celebrating long before it happens. See, when it is revealed to me, and/or at the time that I accept by faith what God has promised, it is then that I fully celebrate, because I walk by faith not by sight. My initial celebration may be weeks, months, or even years before I see the physical manifestation of what God has said, and what I believed would come to pass, but it doesn't stop me from a NOW celebration.

As I mentioned earlier, we as believers must walk by faith not by sight; those who do not believe walk by sight and not by faith. The bible indicates that signs shall follow those who believe. Therefore, the signs are not for the believer but for the nonbeliever. The signs help the nonbeliever to rejoice/ celebrate, and believe in what the believer has previously testified to be true about our God.

Now, of course, walking by faith is not always easy, but regardless of the challenges it may present, it is something that we must do in order to eventually help nonbelievers to open their eyes of understanding. After all…

Romans 8:19 *"For the earnest expectation of the creature waiteth for the manifestation of the sons of God."* (KJV)

We must walk by faith, regardless of the challenges…

2 Corinthians 4:17-18 Vs. 17 ***"For our light affliction, which is but for a moment, worketh for us a far more exceeding and eternal weight of glory;"*** **Vs. 18** *"While we look not at the things which are seen, but at the things which are not seen: for the things which are seen are temporal; but the things which are not seen are eternal."*

(KJV)

Though it is challenging, as a believer we must keep moving, because we are making an impact on our family, our friends, our community, our country, and our world. And when we have completed this walk/ life of faith, we will be able to say as the Apostle Paul has said…

2 Timothy 4:7-8 Vs. 7 *"__I have fought a good fight, I have finished my course, I have kept the faith:__" **Vs. 8** "Henceforth there is laid up for me a crown of righteousness, which the Lord, the righteous judge, shall give me at that day: and not to me only, but unto all them also that love his appearing."* (KJV)

Around 2001, I was invited to go with a friend/ colleague to a conference that she was preaching at in Washington D.C. While at the conference, my friend was introduced to preach and before she did, she asked the host to allow me to do a quick sermonette before she got up. Being taught to always be ready to preach, I got up and read the scripture from Matthew 21:1-10. This was the scripture that is traditionally referred to as Jesus's "triumphal entry" into Jerusalem. This entry was the lead up to His giving of His life through death on the cross at Calvary.

Without going through the full sermonette, allow me to just cut to the chase of the message. The text that centralized the message was **Matthew 21:10** *"And when he was come into Jerusalem, **all the city was moved, saying, Who is this?**"* (KJV) This scripture ultimately speaks of those in Jerusalem at the time of Jesus's entry into the city, all of whom were moved. They had likely either heard of or heard from Jesus, or had known Jesus at some point during one of His travels to and around Jerusalem. They likely knew of some of the things Jesus had done, perhaps maybe had known Him since childhood. Yet when He entered into Jerusalem this time, arrayed in the way that the prophet Zechariah spoke of in Zechariah 9:9 *(more than 500 years before)*, the bible says that they were **all moved**, and said **who is this**? It's like the people knew, but yet didn't know who He was.

See, when you finally see Jesus for who He is, this changes your perspective of everything you thought you knew. The remarkable thing about this event is that everyone in the city was moved; then again, this is the power of Jesus. And the kicker of this is that if you keep Jesus in your heart and in your actions, then you, too, will cause people to be moved and say, who is this? And when they ask, you can simply say, "It's God in me."

<u>THANKS FOR READING</u>

<u>PLEASE GIVE YOUR TESTIMONY</u>

THE END

www.ingramcontent.com/pod-product-compliance
Lightning Source LLC
Chambersburg PA
CBHW071423150726
48000CB00001B/450